Child Abuse

About the series . . .

Series Editor: Alan E. Kazdin, Yale University

The Sage series in **Developmental Clinical Psychology and Psychiatry** is uniquely designed to serve several needs of the field. While the primary focus is on childhood psychopathology, the series also offers monographs prepared by experts in clinical child psychology, child psychiatry, child development, and related disciplines. The series draws upon multiple disciplines, as well as diverse views within a given discipline.

In this series . . .

Child Abuse
Implications for Child Development and Psychopathology

David A. Wolfe

Volume 10.
Developmental Clinical Psychology and Psychiatry

SAGE PUBLICATIONS
The Publishers of Professional Social Science
Newbury Park   London   New Delhi

To Darrell and Eleanor

For information address:

SAGE Publications, Inc.
2111 West Hillcrest Drive
Newbury Park, California 91320

SAGE Publications Ltd.
28 Banner Street
London EC1Y 8QE
England

SAGE Publications India Pvt. Ltd.
M-32 Market
Greater Kailash I
New Delhi 110 048 India

Printed in the United States of America

Library of Congress Cataloging-in-Publication Data

Main entry under title:

Wolfe, David A.
    Child abuse.

    (Developmental clinical psychology and psychiatry ;
v. 10)
    Bibliography: p.
    1. Child abuse.   2. Child development.   3. Parent
and child.   4. Child psychopathology.   I. Title.
II. Series. [DNLM: 1. Child Abuse.   2. Child Develop-
ment.   3. Psychopathology.   W1 DE997NC v.10 /
WA 320 W855e]
HV6626.5.W58   1987   362.7′044   87-16553
ISBN 0-8039-2832-7
ISBN 0-8039-2833-5 (pbk.)

THIRD PRINTING, 1989

CONTENTS

SERIES EDITOR'S INTRODUCTION

Interest in child development and adjustment is by no means new. Yet only recently has the study of children benefited from advances in both clinical and scientific research. Advances in the social and biological sciences, the emergence of disciplines and subdisciplines that focus exclusively on childhood and adolescence, and greater appreciation of the impact of such influences as the family, peers, and school have helped accelerate research on developmental psychopathology. Apart from interest in the study of child development and adjustment for its own sake, the need to address clinical problems of adulthood naturally draws one to investigate precursors in childhood and adolescence.

Within a relatively brief period, the study of psychopathology among children and adolescents has proliferated considerably. Several different professional journals, annual book series, and handbooks devoted entirely to the study of children and adolescents and their adjustment document the proliferation of work in the field. Nevertheless, there is a paucity of resource material that presents information in an authoritative, systematic, and disseminable fashion. There is a need within the field to convey the latest developments and to represent different disciplines, approaches, and conceptual views to the topics of childhood and adolescent adjustment and maladjustment.

The Sage series *Developmental Clinical Psychology and Psychiatry* is designed to serve uniquely several needs of the field. The series encompasses individual monographs prepared by experts in the fields of clinical child psychology, child psychiatry, child development, and related disciplines. The primary focus is on developmental psychopathology, which here refers broadly to the diagnosis, assessment, treatment, and prevention of problems that arise in the period from infancy through adolescence. A working assumption of the series is that understanding, identifying, and treating problems of youth must draw upon multiple disciplines and diverse views within a given discipline.

The task for individual contributors is to present the latest theory and research on various topics including specific types of dysfunction, diagnostic and treatment approaches, and special problem areas that affect adjustment. Core topics within clinical work are addressed by the series. Authors are asked to bridge potential theory, research, and clinical practice, and to outline the current status and future directions. The goals of the series and the tasks presented to individual contributors are demanding. We have been extremely fortunate in recruiting leaders in the fields who have been able to translate their recognized scholarship and expertise into highly readable works on contemporary topics.

The present monograph, *Child Abuse: Implications for Child Development and Psychopathology,* is devoted to a topic of major social and clinical significance. Dr. David A. Wolfe, who has made major contributions to this area of research, has completed a highly integrative and scholarly treatise. The present book reviews a vast array of findings regarding the diverse facets of abuse and characteristics of children, parents, and families with which abuse is associated. Different explanations of abuse are considered and models are offered to suggest new conceptualizations and avenues of research. The book notes the complexity of the phenomena to which abuse refers; in the process of outlining research and theory, Dr. Wolfe dispels misconceptions about who abuses and why. In the process of clarifying our understanding of abuse, the present monograph illuminates a number of important areas regarding child development and reciprocal influences of children and parents.

—Alan E. Kazdin, Ph.D.
Series Editor

PREFACE

The child abuse literature is growing at a rapid pace and is quickly outdating many of our previously held beliefs. When public attention was first drawn to this problem its causes were assumed to be deeply rooted in the personality of the individual. Then nationwide epidemiological studies of child abuse drew our attention toward the chronic turmoil created by socioeconomic stress, which may pressure some predisposed individuals to react with violence. Most recently, we have explained abusive behavior in relation to social learning and developmental processes that shape the behavior of family members, such as the bidirectional influences that parents and children have on one another, and emotional and cognitive processes underlying anger and aggression. In looking back, a great deal of progress has been made toward understanding the major causes of this widespread phenomenon. In this book I intend to convince readers of the need to look at child abuse not only in terms of its causes, but also in terms of its psychological impact on the victims.

Problems in the parent-child relationship are a predominant concern to those who study methods of child socialization. Child abuse encompasses many of the blatant and insidious aspects of such problems, yet these considerations have only recently received the attention of social scientists. The significance of abuse from the standpoint of the impact on the child is not defined by a singular act, or even a series of abusive acts. Rather, child abuse must be considered within its entire social context, both in an attempt to find its causes and cures, and also in an attempt to understand its seemingly pervasive impact on child development.

An understanding of child abuse requires a familiarity with child development and socialization processes, learning principles vis-à-vis family interactions, and normative and nonnormative sources of anger and arousal. Accordingly, definitions and explanations of child abuse that are most relevant to understanding its psychological impact on children's development are emphasized throughout this book, in preference to descriptive or legal definitions. Because of the tremendous significance of socialization practices upon developmental outcomes, the different styles of parenting (both desirable and undesirable) are allotted a sizable proportion of discussion in the introductory chapters. From this foundation, we turn to a more in-depth focus on processes occurring within the individual (both adults and children), the family, and the community that contribute toward the development of severe conflict and abuse.

In writing this book, I have tried to avoid misrepresenting the perpetrators and victims of abuse as belonging to a homogeneous, singular grouping of adults and children. *Child abuse* refers to more than physical injuries—the term encompasses a compilation of significant events, both chronic and acute, that interact with the child's ongoing development to interrupt, alter, or impair his or her psychological development. Thus we are recognizing more and more that abusive parents may possess a wide range of intellectual, emotional, familial, and behavioral differences that interact with current environmental demands to lead to this pattern of abusive behavior. Findings suggest that child abuse is a major symptom of adaptational failure, mostly on the part of the involved adult but to some extent on the part of social and cultural agents responsible for family socialization as well. Prevention-oriented activities therefore are a valuable strategy for reducing the extent and severity of family-related problems, such as providing assistance in family planning, preparation for parenthood, and education and support services for disadvantaged families.

My own work with abusive and distressed families led to a growing concern that we, as mental health professionals, were missing the core issue affecting abused children most significantly. Perhaps because we have seldom experienced firsthand the vast ramifications of parental abuse or related mistreatment, we tend to focus on the more obviously disruptive aspects of abuse, such as physical injuries or disturbing child behavior problems. Yet as I began to consider more of the emotional consequences to the child I saw a connection between the experiences of abused children and the experiences of other victims of violence or personal exploitation. This connection is based on experiences of victimization, which we are only beginning to understand from a psychological standpoint. The implications of considering how abusive socialization practices affect children's views of themselves and others offer a number of important new directions for research and clinical efforts with this population.

An important cautionary note regarding the state of the child abuse literature should be raised. A disturbingly large proportion of the studies reporting on this topic are generalizable to abusive *mothers* only. Although our present data base on child abuse has grown tremendously over the past 10 years, it appears to be highly skewed in its overall sampling. As a case in point, Bradley (1986) reviewed all of the published studies on this topic that used well-defined samples of abusers and found that 76% of the studies included only female subjects. Many of the studies that included males, furthermore, reported a high ratio of female to male participants. This high percentage of female-only participants is particularly alarming in light of the fact that three out of five reports of physical abuse nationwide involve males. The extent to which the results to date are representative therefore remains uncertain and problematic. This finding, of course, is not confined to research on child abuse alone but rather is a pervasive problem throughout the psychological literature on parenting problems (Caplan, 1986). Conceivably, the general conclusions derived from findings with abusive mothers will be maintained once males are included, yet it is also to be anticipated that some significant discrepancies will emerge from future efforts involving both sexes.

I am gratefully indebted to the many students and colleagues who have contributed their ideas and their time toward the completion of this project. My wife Vicky deserves special commendation not only for her emotional support, but also for her conceptual and editorial finesse that was brought to bear throughout the stages of writing. Jack Sandler and Jeffrey Kelly merit special thanks for providing excellent training and supervision in working with distressed families in Florida and Mississippi. My research colleague and friend, Peter Jaffe, has also been instrumental in sharing ideas and energy from the beginning of my involvement with families in London, Ontario. Special appreciation is extended to the administration and staff of Family and Children's Services of London/Middlesex County (Children's Aid Society of Ontario), who have shared with me their expertise and professional commitment to the remediation of child maltreatment. Finally, my involvement in research with abusive families was made possible in part by grants from the Medical Research Council of Canada and the Ontario Mental Health Foundation.

—D.A.W.

1

ESTABLISHING THE DIMENSIONS OF CHILD MALTREATMENT

TWENTIETH-CENTURY DEVELOPMENTS IN AWARENESS AND REPORTING

Acts ranging from extreme parental indifference and neglect to physical and sexual abuse of children have been commonplace throughout history. Harsh and abusive treatment, in particular, has been culturally sanctioned for the discipline or education of children, the pleasing of certain gods, the expelling of evil spirits, or as a suitable cure for unruly child behavior (Radbill, 1968). For many generations, the implicit societal viewpoint that children are the exclusive property and responsibility of their parents was undaunted by any countermovement to seek more humane treatment for children who suffered from improper care. A parent's prerogative to enforce child obedience, for example, was endorsed by Massachusetts's passage of the "Stubborn Child Act" in the early 1600s, whereby a rebellious or stubborn child could be petitioned by his or her parents to be put to death (Fraser, 1976; cited in Kelly, 1983). It has become increasingly apparent that excessive and abusive child-rearing practices are not recent phenomena, nor are they associated with any single cultural heritage.

Legal and social precedents for intervention on behalf of maltreated children (that is, child victims of physical and sexual abuse, emotional cruelty, or severe parental neglect) slowly became established in the early part of the twentieth century. The first of these precedents was the passage of the Social Security Act in the 1930s, which made child protection a public responsibility, thereby diminishing the need for voluntary agencies such as the Societies for Prevention of Cruelty to Children. Official recognition of the problem of children in need of protection spurred research investigations that established for the first time that some types of physical injuries to children (e.g., subdural hematomas and fractures of long bones) were the result of willful trauma inflicted by their parents (Caffey, 1946; Silverman, 1953). Soon thereafter, public awareness and concerns were fomented by descriptions of the "battered child syndrome" (Kempe, Silverman, Steele, Droegenmueller, & Silver, 1962), leading to the drafting of model child abuse legislation in the early 1960s.

Over the following decade, mandatory reporting laws became established in all states and provinces in North America, paving the way for large-scale surveys and epidemiological studies of the problem of child maltreatment (American Humane Association [AHA], 1984). Concurrently, social casework joined forces with the medical profession to embrace the view of child maltreatment as a medical and psychiatric problem, although specific diagnostic information and treatment directions were still lacking. The nationwide survey of Gil (1970) is often cited as the most detailed investigation to emerge from these early efforts to define and describe this problem. Gil reviewed every available case of physical child abuse reported in the United States through legal channels in 1967 and 1968 (over 20,000 cases) and documented for the first time that a high proportion of abused children were members of multistressed, multiproblem families. The effects of poverty, in particular, were highlighted as playing a significant role in the etiology of abuse. Additional large-scale probes into the social causes of abuse immediately followed, which continued to highlight the relationship between many forms of family violence and dysfunction (such as spouse abuse, child abuse, incest, and delinquency) and sociodemographic conditions such as poverty, unemployment, social and physical isolation from community resources, and overcrowding (Smith, Hanson, & Noble, 1974; Straus, Gelles, & Steinmetz, 1980).

Social scientists and practitioners were initially slow to respond to this problem, due most likely to the difficulty of studying behavior that is illegal, occurs at low frequency in the privacy of the home, and is not viewed as atypical or inappropriate by the persons who perform it (Wolfe, in press). However, professional involvement dramatically increased following the creation in 1974 of the U.S. National Center on Child Abuse and Neglect under the Federal Child Abuse Prevention and Treatment Act (P.L. 93-247), which resulted in over $50 million being spent on research, demonstration, and evaluation activities between 1974 and 1980. Despite justifiable criticism that research in child abuse and neglect has been of limited scope and design (Besharov, 1982; Smith, 1984), we have seen a pronounced expansion of our reporting, understanding, and treatment of this problem in recent years.

Violence between family members has begun to emerge from its cloistered position to become a major societal concern. Public awareness of this problem has greatly increased over the past past decade— 90% of the American population now consider child abuse to be a serious national problem, compared to 10% in 1976 (Magnuson, 1983). In parallel, the number of official reports of child abuse and neglect (combined) has risen sharply from 416,000 in 1976 to over 929,000 in 1982 (AHA, 1984). Among these victims of child maltreatment, approximately one-half million were known to have been physically abused by their caregivers during 1982 (based on reports of "abuse only" or "combined abuse and neglect"). These figures on the number of officially reported cases are considered to be only a fraction of the expected total, however. Based on a nationwide survey of family behavior, Straus et al. (1980) estimate that 14% of all children (140/1000) are subject to abusive treatment each year.

In this chapter, we will review some of the major developments in defining and describing abusive families that have arisen from recent efforts to understand the social and cultural nature of child abuse.

DEFINING DIFFERENT
TYPES OF CHILD MALTREATMENT

The existence of an adequate definition of child abuse and neglect is central to the entire system of detection, prevention, and service delivery to problem families. Communities must identify those children and families in need of help, while simultaneously educating all community members in the currently acceptable and unacceptable forms of child rearing. However, despite public outcry and disdain for child maltreatment, efforts to define child abuse and neglect have been fraught with controversy and shortcomings. This controversy exists in part because the nature of child maltreatment does not lend itself to clear definitions that apply to each new situation without considerable discretion.

Different definitions of child abuse may be adopted by an organization, government, community, or investigator in order to serve a particular purpose for that group or individual. Thus municipalities often adopt a legally based definition that focuses largely on evidential criteria (to prove or disprove the act of abuse), whereas caseworkers (who are mandated to investigate accusations of maltreatment) may weigh other discretionary criteria more heavily for determining their course of action, such as the parent's remorse, family resources, and the child's need for protection. An additional approach to defining child maltreatment focuses on the social and psychological implications of abuse for the child's development, which serves a purpose that is particularly relevant to social science research. These definitional approaches are reviewed briefly, to compare and contrast their value and shortcomings in relation to child maltreatment.

Legal and Descriptive Definitions
of Abuse and Neglect

Legal statutes have attempted over the past three decades to define the minimal criteria acceptable for child care, with provisions for social or legal intervention specified under certain circumstances such as nonaccidental injuries or inadequate medical attention. The general definition of child abuse that has emerged in conjunction with these statutes emphasizes the presence of nonaccidental injuries as a result of acts of commission (physical assault) or omission (failure to protect) by caretakers (Kempe & Helfer, 1972; NIMH, 1977). Thus statutorily defined physical abuse often refers most directly to a condition of physical harm to the child, but also indirectly covers any "child in need of protection" (that is, a child whose life, health, or safety may be endangered by the conduct of his or her caregiver). Legal definitions are weighted heavily toward the overt consequences of abuse (e.g., bruises, welts, broken limbs), yet they serve an important purpose for delineating minimum community standards of child care. From a legal perspective, civil protective legislation is often considered to be a therapeutic approach to defining and preventing child abuse, in contrast to the more punitive Criminal Code provisions prohibiting assault and related bodily offenses (Pamenter-Potvin, 1985). These latter provisions are more commonly pursued in extreme and serious cases of physical injury to a child.

A further definition of those behaviors that are considered to constitute child maltreatment may be formulated on the basis of caseworkers' investigations. A look at the types of acts that are most commonly reported to child protective service agencies provides a practical understanding of maltreatment terminology, incidence, and demographics based on empirically derived incident reports.

Most notably, a composite profile of reported maltreatment from 1976 to 1982 (compiled from national statistics by the American Humane Association, 1984) reveals a fairly consistent pattern: 64% of these children experienced "deprivation of necessities" by their caregivers, such as neglecting to provide nourishment, clothing, shelter, health care, education, supervision, or causing failure to thrive. An additional 25% were the victims of physical injuries, which have been defined under two major categories: *major physical injuries* (comprising about one-eighth of the cases), which include brain damage/skull fracture, subdural hemorrhage or hematoma, bone fracture, dislocation/sprains, internal injuries, poisonings, burns/scalds, severe cuts/lacerations/bruises/welts, or related injuries; and *minor physical injuries* (comprising the remainder of the cases), which include twisting/shaking, minor cuts/bruises/welts, or similar injuries that do not constitute a substantial risk to the life and well-being of the child.

In addition to the sizable categories of abuse and neglect, emotional and sexual maltreatment of children have received greater attention and recognition in recent years. Emotional maltreatment, a loosely defined category referring to behavior on the part of the caretaker that causes low self-esteem of the child, undue fear or anxiety, or other damage to the child's emotional well-being, accounted for 17% of all nationwide reports. Sexual abuse, which includes the involvement of a child in any sexual act or situation such as incest, exploitation, intercourse, and molestation, climbed from 3% in 1976 to 7% of the reports in 1982, a trend that appears to reflect the growing recognition of the severity of this form of child maltreatment (see Finkelhor, 1984; Wolfe & Wolfe, in press).

These data from reported cases should dispel the public's image of child maltreatment as involving severe physical injuries to the child. That is, a sizable majority of the physical abuse cases (88%) were classified by caseworkers as involving minor physical injuries to the child. It is also highly significant that nearly two-thirds of the total population of maltreated children experienced deprivation of necessities, often typified by chronic environmental deprivation, parental disinterest, and similar conditions that do not foster healthy child development. Furthermore, many children experience more than one form of maltreatment (illustrated by the finding that 46% of neglect reports also involve some form of suspected abuse; AHA, 1984). Despite the overlap in abuse and neglect reports, however, most investigators argue the importance of considering these phenomena as somewhat distinct forms of parental and familial dysfunction (see Bousha & Twentyman, 1984; Herrenkohl, Herrenkohl, & Egolf, 1983). The significance of such distinctions is revealed most noticeably in relation to the impact on the child's adjustment and development (see Chapter 5).

Although evidence of physical injury to the child remains a critical definitional factor, more and more emphasis is being placed on the circumstances and nature of the act (as opposed to the consequences) in differentiating abuse from nonabuse (Smith, 1984). In practice, the process of deciding whether or not a specific incident constitutes physical abuse typically involves two judgments (Giovannoni & Becerra, 1979): (1) the extent to which the act was sufficiently deviant to warrant child protection (such as using a fist, weapon, or dangerous object to control the child), and (2) the dangerousness of the current situation, as determined by ambient stress factors that may affect the parent-child relationship (such as parental complaints of "losing control" with the child; severe economic or family instability). Consequently, we must recognize that whether or not a family will be labeled as abusive is often based on the subjective judgment of professionals rather than objective definitional criteria (Kelly, 1983). An absolute standard for judging the acceptability of cultural child-rearing methods clearly is neither possible nor desirable. Child abuse definitions therefore must continue to evolve in response to the difficulties of inferring intentionality, the possible role of the child in shaping parental aggression, and the sociocultural context of parenting methods (Parke, 1977).

Social Science Definitions

The legal-social definition of child abuse has shaped theory, research, and social intervention regarding this phenomenon over the past two decades. This definition places a major emphasis on parental deviance and wrongdoing, thereby directing our focus predominantly on the implicit intent to inflict harm or the incapability of the parent to protect the child from harm. Yet the statistics above reveal that the vast majority of physically abusive incidents are of a minor nature, typically occurring in the context of discipline (Herrenkohl et al., 1983; Kadushin & Martin, 1981). This conceptualization of physical abuse as impulsive yet not necessarily malicious forms a major basis for contending that abusive parents are not marked by major forms of psychopathology but rather demonstrate critical deficits within the boundless context of parenting (discussed in Chapters 3 and 4). Thus more and more emphasis by social scientists has been placed upon the importance of social and familial variables, such as antecedents to abuse, the type of act committed, and the intensity of the reaction, that define child abuse within the context of child-rearing norms (Burgess, 1979; Friedman, Sandler, Hernandez, & Wolfe, 1981; Parke & Collmer, 1975).

Apart from the physical consequences of abuse, social scientists have been concerned about the social-psychological implications of maltreatment upon the child's development. The psychological nature of maltreatment, such as the intensity, chronicity, or seriousness of the child's victimization experiences, is more difficult to record and is suspected to be more damaging to the child than physical injuries. Although a social-psychological definition often is not fully compatible with legal statutes and similar criteria outlining the global parameters of caregivers' rights and choices, such a definition is highly worthwhile for studying the impact of abuse on the child and the family. A social-psychological definition of child abuse emphasizes the nature of the socialization process that permits the use of violence as a means of interpersonal control and problem solving (LaRose & Wolfe, in press; Parke, 1977).

Child abuse, according to this perspective, can be viewed as an extreme disturbance of child rearing, which is to say it is not necessarily an individual disorder or psychological disturbance. Abusive families are ones in which the usual balance between positive and negative interactions and between discipline and emotional bonding has not been achieved. Thus they are families that have ceased to function as facilitators of the child's social and cognitive development and as an arena for socialization (Maccoby & Martin, 1983). Furthermore, child abuse is often enmeshed in other serious family problems (such as parents who are alcoholic, depressed, antisocial, or are experiencing major child conduct problems), all of which are related to some degree to negative developmental outcomes. Therefore, the socialization practices that abusive and other distressed families have in common should receive the majority of our attention in defining this problem.

A PROFILE OF
SOCIODEMOGRAPHIC RISK FACTORS

Epidemiological findings of abusive families provide a critical base for understanding the causes and consequences of physical abuse. Such studies provide a *descriptive profile* of this phenomenon, illuminating many of the cultural forces that surround child-rearing methods and that contribute indirectly to parental aggression. Epidemiological variables associated with abuse, such as low income, unemployment, and family stability, provide important "markers" for identifying high-risk groups in society, which allow for subsequent investigations into the causal mechanisms relating these variables to abusive parenting. We will look at several of these major factors in relation to children, parents, and families, based predominantly upon findings from the National Study on the Incidence and Severity of Child Abuse and Neglect (National Center on Child Abuse and Neglect [NCCAN], 1981) and the National Study on Child Neglect and Abuse Reporting (AHA, 1984).

Abused Children

Certain child characteristics have been identified that appear to enhance the probability of certain forms of maltreatment. In general, the child victims of abuse and neglect are relatively young (average age of 7.4 years), in comparison to the average age of all U.S. children (9.4 years). Neglect is most often reported when children are quite young (infancy and toddlerhood), with incidence declining with age. In contrast, reports of sexual and emotional maltreatment occur most frequently among older, school-aged children and adolescents. Physical abuse affects a sizable proportion of all age groups. The highest rate of physical *injury,* however, is found among the older children (12-17 years of age). Although this latter finding seems surprising in light of the public image of this problem centering on small children, it corresponds with increasing parent-child conflict that occurs during adolescent development.

With the exception of sexual abuse (where females comprise 85% of the victims), boys and girls are reported at approximately the same rate for physical abuse and neglect. Race of the victim has also been investigated through these reporting figures, indicating that the percentage of black and white children is representative of the U.S. population at large. However, the *profile* of reports made on black children is distinctly different from the overall group. That is, black families have been characterized by more neglect and slightly less physical and sexual abuse, whereas white families have been characterized by more abuse or combined abuse/neglect. In addition, concerns expressed in earlier studies about a possible reporting bias that would lead to blacks being reported more often than whites have not been confirmed by these recent analyses. One inference drawn from this finding is that reports are now being labeled more correctly—in the past, a concerned individual may have reported "abuse" even though neglect was the primary issue.

Abusive Parents

In 97% of reported cases of child maltreatment parents are the perpetrators, with a large percentage being natural parents. It is noteworthy that natural parents, overall, are reported for less sexual abuse and more neglect than are other caregivers (such as stepparents, relatives, foster parents, and guardians), who commit more sexual and physical abuse.

Abusive parents often began their families at a younger age than did other families in the population, with many being in their teens at the birth of their first child. There are also more female than male caregivers reported for all forms of child maltreatment when considered together (60.8% female, 39.2% male), which presumably reflects the predominance of female-headed households and child-rearing responsibilities. However, the sex of the perpetrator is significant in terms of the *type* of maltreatment, a fact that has been overlooked in part by the lack of investigations involving males. Males are associated with more major and minor *physical injury* (that is, physical abuse), the vast majority of sexual abuse, and less neglect than females. For example, based on 1982 statistics from the National Study, 21.6% of the total sample of maltreated children were physically abused by a male, as compared to 14.6% who were physically abused by females. Thus the perpetrator of *physical abuse,* in particular, was approximately 1.5 times more likely to be a male than a female. The finding of greater neglect among females may be linked to the greater likelihood of adverse socioeconomic factors, that is, when only the mother is present in the home, economic difficulties are more prevalent and child neglect emerges as the most common form of maltreatment.

Abusive Families

Child abuse and neglect appear to be mediated by several major environmental conditions, of which socioeconomic status (SES) plays a significant role. Low SES, typically defined as family incomes below the poverty mark, underemployment, and less education, has proven to be a powerful aggregate variable associated with negative outcomes at several points in child development. Impoverished pregnant women are prone to be undernourished, receive poor prenatal care, are exposed to more toxic agents, and consequently suffer more complications at delivery. After delivery, their children are exposed to greater postnatal risks, such as malnutrition, injury, and lack of stimulation, that are commonly associated with ongoing poverty and family disadvantage. Thus it is widely accepted that lower socioeconomic level can serve as a significant risk factor to child development and child maltreatment, whereas higher SES can serve as an ameliorating, protective factor (Masten & Garmezy, 1985).

In relation to these concerns, it is perhaps not surprising to find that a strong relationship has consistently emerged between reports of child maltreatment and poverty. In other words, there is a consensus that child maltreatment is related to economic inequality and occurs disproportionately more often among economically and socially disadvantaged families (Pelton, 1978; NCCAN, 1981). When compared to all U.S. families with children, for example, maltreated children are twice as likely to live in a single-parent, female-headed household, four times as likely to be supported by public assistance, and are affected by numerous stress factors that impinge upon family functioning, such as health problems, alcohol abuse, and wife battering (AHA, 1984). The consistency and multiple-source derivatives of this conclusion support the fact that there is a real and strong relationship between economic difficulties and child maltreatment, one that does not appear to result from bias in reporting.

However, it is essential to recognize that child maltreatment does occur in varying degrees at all socioeconomic levels, and that the role of socioeconomic factors may be considerably different for abuse and neglect. That is, the large proportion of families characterized by neglect may skew the profile of family SES factors, and thus disguise the status of physically abusive families. In a comparative analysis of abuse and neglect reports across the United States (Schene, 1983; cited in AHA, 1984), neglectful families were considerably below the national average on several sociodemographic indicators (47.6% of the neglectful families versus 17.3% of all U.S. families were receiving public assistance; 44.1% versus 6.5% were unemployed); however, abusive families were closer to the U.S. average (that is, 33.7% were receiving public assistance; 23.7% were unemployed). Further strengthening the ties between neglect and SES, as compared to abuse and SES, caseworkers investigating reports of child maltreatment noted the presence of significantly more stress factors for neglectful than abusive families, such as problems in their economic/living conditions (63.8% of neglectful versus 39.9% of abusive), inadequate housing (18.8% versus 7.0%), and insufficient income (7.3% versus 5.5%).

IS THE RATE OF CHILD ABUSE INCREASING?

There has been a significant increase in the total number of child maltreatment cases reported nationwide to child protective service agencies each year since 1976, with over twice as many reports in recent years than was true 10 years ago. At a practical level, this increase places a considerable burden on the child welfare system's ability to respond to these increasing allegations of abuse and neglect. At a more theoretical level, however, this increase in reporting raises other important questions: Are we merely "uncovering" a larger proportion of the problem that has always existed or are proportionately more parents actually abusing or neglecting their children now than before?

In support of the argument that a larger proportion of cases are being uncovered, one can make note of the fact that a number of factors have occurred over the past decade that affect reporting but not actual incidence. For example, the allocation of more federal money, improvements in intake and legal procedures, 24-hour hotlines, and massive public awareness campaigns should account for a significant rise in the number of reported cases. But the researchers who monitor these figures at the American Humane Association's national headquarters raise another very important countersuggestion regarding the relationship between incidence and reporting. The seven-year period (1976-1982) represented a time of economic recession and high unemployment, factors that have been strongly linked to an increased incidence of child maltreatment. Yet the *rate* of reporting during this period actually slowed (between 1976 and 1977 there was a 24% increase in reporting, whereas between 1980 and 1981 there was an 8% increase).

Epidemiological researchers suspect that the same economic conditions that affect individuals may affect the child welfare system as a whole, forcing staff layoffs, increased caseloads, and a priority system of case management. Consequently, the number of new cases that make it into the system may begin to level off. In other words, if funding for child protective services had kept pace with the suspected demand during the late 1970s and early 1980s (arising from economic hardships), the official reporting statistics most likely would have revealed a considerably larger number of cases. Therefore, we may conclude that the number of families at risk for child abuse and neglect appears to be on the rise, in conjunction with increasing economic hardship that affects children's lives. This conclusion is supported by a report from the House of Representatives Select Committee on Children, Youth and Families (1983; cited in AHA, 1984), which indicated that the economic status of children—especially minority children—has clearly deteriorated over the past decade.

2

VARIATIONS IN FAMILY SOCIALIZATION PRACTICES

Child-rearing practices are influenced by numerous cultural and situational factors that determine the level of conflict or cooperation in the emerging parent-child relationship. From a socialization perspective, child abuse is viewed not as an isolated social phenomenon or a psychological impairment of the parent but rather as the product of socialization practices that sanction the use of violence and power-assertive techniques with family members. This socialization process, it is argued, is largely responsible for establishing the "norms" of acceptable or tolerable child-rearing methods in a given community or region.

In order to understand how families become socialized into abusive patterns of child treatment, it is important to consider the impact of cultural, community, and familial influences on child-rearing patterns. In this chapter, North American child-rearing patterns will be explored along with their unique influences on child development. We also examine how children's behavior and characteristics can influence parental socialization techniques in both desirable and undesirable ways. The development of the parent-child relationship is then analyzed from a systems perspective that integrates individual, familial, and cultural factors affecting socialization practices among both abusive and nonabusive families. This perspective establishes the foundation for understanding the development of severe parent-child conflict and abuse, which is reviewed in detail in Chapter 3.

CHILD-REARING PATTERNS AND THEIR
INFLUENCE ON CHILD DEVELOPMENT

A parent who abuses a child is often viewed by community members as being quite different or distinct from other nonabusive parents. That is, such behavior is so inconceivable, so heinous to some that a false dichotomy inadvertently surfaces to separate and define "abusive" parents in relation to "normal" parents. As with similar dichotomies, the negative characteristics associated with the problem are ascribed to all persons identified as abusive; likewise, the positive characteristics of nurturing parents are assumed to be absent in abusive parents and possessed by all those who are not abusive. An assumption underlying this dichotomous viewpoint is that parental behavior and the motivation to interact positively with children is a natural, universal phenomenon that is intrinsically based in the best interests of the child. Those who do not possess this ability or desire presumably may fall into the category of either "abusive" or "neglectful," and can be identified and labeled as "abnormal" or psychopathic. Clearly, this is not the case if one looks at the different styles of parenting that are commonly practiced in each community. Variations in socialization practices occur normally in relation to child, family, and situational events. Some variations are nurturant, whereas others are viewed as inappropriate and undesirable.

An alternative conceptualization that avoids the false dichotomy between normal and abusive parenting practices is based upon a continuum model of parenting behavior (see Bell & Harper, 1977; Burgess, 1979). At one end of the continuum are those practices considered to be most severe and abusive toward the child, and at the other extreme are methods that promote the child's social, emotional, and intellectual development. Accordingly, child abuse can be viewed in terms of the *degree to which a parent uses negative, inappropriate control strategies with his or her child.* Rather then being a symptom of a parental disorder, many forms of child abuse are viewed as the extreme to which a parent goes in disciplining his or her child. The continuum model also serves to highlight parenting styles that may fail to meet the child's needs, such as a lack of physical affection or verbal praise, or unclear communication from the parent. Viewing child abuse as a continuum of child-rearing practices is not intended to negate or diminish the seriousness of the consequences to the child; rather, it is intended to draw attention toward those aspects of abuse that resemble "typical" parenting methods except in terms of their degree.

Dimensions of Parental Behavior: Toward a Classification of Parenting Styles

Much of the research on child-rearing patterns has sought to identify characteristics that clearly distinguish different parenting styles in terms of their effects on child development. The last two decades of research on parenting practices have produced significant advances in our knowledge of how dissimilar approaches to child rearing can emerge from the interaction of two fundamental dimensions of parenting, labeled *demandingness* and *responsiveness*. Demandingness is defined as the amount or degree of control the parent attempts to exert over the child, while responsiveness is defined as the frequency of parenting interactions (both positive and negative) that are child-centered versus parent-centered (that is, the degree to which the parent behaves in response to the needs and behavior shown by the child).

This two-dimensional classification of parenting patterns results in a fourfold scheme of parenting "styles," shown in Figure 2.1, which has important applications for the definition and study of child abuse and related forms of inappropriate parenting behavior (Maccoby & Martin, 1983). Parents who are both demanding and child-centered in their responsiveness (that is, sensitive to the child's abilities and needs) are referred to as *Authoritative* (Baumrind, 1971), as shown in the upper-left corner of Figure 2.1. This style is considered to be the most effective child-rearing approach in terms of enhancing the child's development and reducing parent-child conflict. An authoritative parent often places age-appropriate demands on the child, which are primarily demands for mature behavior, independence, and clear communication. Authoritative parents tend to be more consistent in their disciplinary actions and to rely on a wide choice of parenting techniques to gain child compliance or encourage socialization goals (Baumrind, 1971; Hoffman, 1975). For example, when faced with a child who refuses to sit at the table and eat dinner without disturbing others, the authoritative parent might conceptualize the situation as a learning or socialization opportunity for the child, rather than viewing it solely as an annoyance. Moreover, the authoritative parent will be demanding of the child in a manner that is commensurate with the child's capabilities. If the child is preschool aged, he or she may be requested by the parent to "eat quietly with the family or eat by yourself in the next room." The child's efforts to comply with this statement would be followed by praise and positive attention.

In contrast to the more effective methods noted above, the three other parenting styles represented by the combinations of the demandingness and responsiveness dimensions can lead to problematic parent-child relations that affect normal child development. Parents who are demanding of the child but are rejecting or unresponsive to their children's needs (parent-centered) have been labeled *Authoritarian* (Baumrind, 1971). Parents who demand little of their children yet are

	Accepting, Responsive, *Child-Centered*	*Rejecting, Unresponsive,* *Parent-Centered*
Demanding, *Controlling*	Authoritative, reciprocal; high in bidirectional communication	Authoritarian, power assertive
Undemanding, *Low in Control* *Attempts*	Indulgent	Neglecting; ignoring, indifferent, uninvolved

SOURCE: E. E. Maccoby & J. A. Martin (1983). Socialization in the context of the family: Parent-child interaction. In E. M. Hetherington (Ed.), *Socialization, personality, and social development* (vol. IV, pp. 1-101). New York: John Wiley. Used by permission.

Figure 2.1:   A Two-Dimensional Classification of Parenting Patterns

extremely child-centered are referred to as *Indulgent,* while those who demand little of their children and are simultaneously unresponsive to them represent the *Neglecting* typology.

Of particular interest to the present topic is the relationship between the Authoritarian style of parenting and child abuse. There is a great deal of overlap in the attitudinal and behavioral correlates of both forms of parenting, leading to speculation that abusive parenting is the clinical extreme of the authoritarian style (LaRose & Wolfe, 1987). Authoritarian parents exhibit an insensitivity to the child's level of ability, interest, or needs that may impair the child's self-esteem or motivation, as exemplified by the parent who offers a young child very little direction or feedback while expecting the child to complete a difficult task. As discussed in Chapter 4, abusive parents are often described in terms similar to the above, albeit at a more intense and extreme level. For example, abusive parents rely heavily on power-assertive techniques (Oldershaw, Walters, & Hall, 1986; Trickett & Kuczynski, 1986) and are often unresponsive to their child's needs (Azar, Robinson, Hekimian, & Twentyman, 1984; Steele & Pollock, 1968).

Authoritarian Parenting Style
and Developmental Impairments

A major problem of authoritarian parenting styles is that overreliance on coercion in child rearing may impair children's development of social competence and moral reasoning. In this child-rearing pattern, parents' demands on their children are not balanced by acceptance of demands from their children, restricting the child's ability to assert his or her needs and participate in the process of rule generation and regulation. Parental authority is relegated to a position of primary importance, and challenges to this authority by the child are duly suppressed by the parent, often through fairly severe forms of punishment.

Several child characteristics have been associated with the authoritarian pattern of parenting. Children of authoritarian parents tend to be less socially competent than their peers, as evidenced by their tendency to withdraw, to avoid taking initiative, and to lack spontaneity, affection, curiosity, and originality (Baldwin, 1948; Baumrind & Black, 1967). Such children also show less evidence of "conscience" and to have an external, rather then internal, orientation in situations involving moral conflict (that is, they perceive the conflict as caused by something or someone other than themselves, and are less likely to admit guilt or self-blame; Hoffman, 1970). Boys from authoritarian families, in particular, seem to show low self-esteem and diminished intellectual performance in comparison to boys from families where greater freedom of choice is exercised (Coopersmith, 1967). These latter findings, in conjunction with related studies of socialization differences among boys and girls, have led to speculation that the negative impact of authoritarian child-rearing may be somewhat stronger for boys than for girls (Maccoby & Martin, 1983). Furthermore, the preponderance of evidence ties children's aggression to inconsistent and/or intensive levels of power-assertion by the parent (see Parke & Slaby, 1983). In brief, the relationship between authoritarian parenting and developmental problems appears significantly strong to merit concern. This relationship becomes even more salient and demonstrative in relation to child abuse, which is explored in greater depth in Chapter 5.

CHILD EFFECTS ON ADULT SOCIALIZATION

In the previous section patterns of parental behavior were described that related to particular child outcomes. This unidirectional viewpoint of the parent-child relationship (that the parent's behavior influences the child's behavior) has been the predominant orientation in the clinical and developmental literature until recently (see Gelfand & Peterson, 1985). However, there is considerable evidence that child and infant characteristics can affect parental behavior as well (see Bell & Harper, 1977), which has important implications for the child's vulnerability to abuse. The manner in which a parent responds to a child may be directly related to mental, physical, or behavioral characteristics of that child, some of which may be congenital or related to developmental handicaps, and others learned (e.g., temper tantrums).

In the following section, findings linking salient child characteristics (such as difficult child behavior and child compliance) to aspects of parental behavior are reviewed, based on nonabusive parent-child samples.

Difficult Infant and Child Behavior

Several studies investigating child effects on adults have uncovered problematic behavior patterns of young children that could elicit negative parental responses. For example, early research by Stevens-Long (1973) indicated that a child's activity level may affect the parent's reactions and disciplinary responses by cueing the adult to increase punishment intensity (a finding that is no surprise to parents of very active children!). Similarly, Patterson (1982) reports that aggressive and disruptive children are at greater risk for harsh punitive reactions from their parents, based on a process of reciprocal escalation in aversive exchanges between the parent and the child. That is, the child may do something that annoys the parent (e.g., hits a sibling), which results in scolding or punishment by the parent. With *nonaggressive* children, the probability that the child will continue with annoying behaviors is reduced by the parent's response; however, with *aggressive* children the probability of continued and escalated coercion is actually increased by parental attempts at discipline (Patterson, 1982).

Further evidence that children's difficult behavior or early temperament patterns influence the type of care received from parents is shown in a recent study by Maccoby, Snow, and Jacklin (reported in Maccoby & Martin, 1983). A group of infants was assessed for temperament (fussing and crying, poor soothability, resistance to routine caretaking operations) at age 12 months and again at 18 months. It is interesting that maternal behavior toward infants was generally unrelated to the infant's level of difficulty at the *initial* assessment. However, the degree of child difficulty appeared to modify maternal behavior over the 12- to 18-month period. Mothers of difficult boys exerted less teaching pressure and appeared to "back away" from socialization efforts.

Furthermore, mothers who initially exerted relatively little teaching pressure at 12 months had sons who became somewhat more difficult in their temperament at 18 months of age. The authors interpret these findings as reflecting the possible origins of a destabilizing process, whereby the parent-child relationship begins to deteriorate in a circular manner—the infant's behavior becomes more difficult, so the parent makes fewer and fewer attempts to manage or teach the infant, and vice versa.

A discussion of child effects on adult socialization must also include some recognition of the *expectancies* that each member develops over time through their relationship. The parent who experiences a difficult infant for several months learns to anticipate such problems before they actually surface. Similarly, the infant or toddler quickly learns to distinguish among different parental cues or behaviors that may lead to desired or unpleasant events. This process of learning what to expect of the other party is important for the development of a stable relationship built on expectations and awareness of the other's behavior. The healthy development of the parent-child relationship may be impeded, however, due to carryover from previous conflict or distress that predominated during an earlier stage in the relationship. For example, a parent may continue to respond to her young child in a negative or inappropriate fashion, even once the child's behavior has developed beyond the early limitations and difficulty experienced during infancy. This parental treatment in turn may serve to perpetuate the child's negative interchanges with the parent and further serve to convince the parent that his or her child will never change. When the child has been "tagged" by the parent as a problem during early childhood, future problems are attributed to the same traits of the child as before.

Parent-Child Interactions in Healthy Families

In contrast to the negative process described above, some children may exhibit appropriate behavior that serves to foster an increasingly positive parent-child relationship over time. These children seem to shape their own environment through their readiness to be socialized, which in turn positively strengthens the parent-child bond (Maccoby & Martin, 1983). It should come as no surprise that favorable adult responses are associated with positive child behavior. Children who express positive affect, have moderate activity levels, respond appropriately to adult instructions and feedback, and use age-appropriate language and social skills clearly are more likely to receive positive attention and reactions from adults (Atwater & Morris, 1979). Such desirable child behavior does not occur by chance or solely because of innate characteristics of the child, however. Rather, it appears that parental *sensitivity* to the child's ongoing state (that is, his or her readiness to comply) is an important factor influencing the child's willingness to cooperate.

This latter conclusion derives from research on children's compliance to parental directives. Compliance is considered to be a critical accomplishment in establishing positive interactions between parent and child. Observations of the manner in which competent parents achieve compliance with their children have indicated that such parents closely monitor the attentional state of their children and adapt the nature of their request according to the child's current state of attention or involvement (Maccoby & Martin, 1983). Before expecting the child to comply to a request, the parent first ensures that the child is oriented to him or her (as opposed to being engrossed in play or some high-interest activity). Thus the initial statement from the parent may be one of orientation (for example, "Let me see what you're playing with, Jimmy"), followed by more specific actions to begin picking up the toys.

The significance of parental sensitivity to the child's attentional state and the child's rate of compliance to parental requests was highlighted in a series of studies reported in Lytton (1980). Parents and their 2½-year-old sons were observed in their home regarding parental behaviors leading to compliance. Parents who consistently enforced the rules in the home, used psychological as opposed to material rewards, and frequently engaged in joint play and cooperative activity with their children had children who were much more cooperative and receptive to parental requests. In essence, the parent and the child ran the show together and shared the role of initiating new activities rather than being one sided (parent-directed only).

In line with Baumrind's concept of authoritative parenting style, Lytton's results support the notion that parental respect for the child's own competence and individuality plays a critical role in developing a healthy parent-child relationship. Other research has similarly shown that parents who use explanations and inductive reasoning with their children attain higher rates of compliance and moral reasoning in their children than those who rely upon power assertion (e.g., physical control) or love withdrawal (Baumrind & Black, 1967; Lytton, 1980).

In brief, a style of cooperation tends to develop reciprocally among parents and children. Parents who are themselves cooperative and attentive to their child's needs and capabilities tend to have children who are similarly cooperative and easier to manage. In sharp contrast, parents who rely upon intrusive and power-assertive methods of control are compromising their future complacency, in that their offspring are more likely to reciprocate in kind with annoying and disruptive behavior, and will fail to acquire the prosocial behaviors that are the goal of their power-assertion attempts. Although it is tempting to say that the predominant direction of influence is from parent to child, it is quite possible that some children are more predisposed than others to establish a cooperative or coercive style of interaction with their parents.

DEVELOPMENTAL PROCESS OF THE
PARENT-CHILD RELATIONSHIP:
AN INTEGRATED MODEL

A major premise of much of the research on child development concerns how deviation at one level (e.g., difficult child temperament) sparks deviant parent and family reactions at other levels (e.g., child discipline). Given the complex nature of child socialization processes, however, the causal direction of these effects is difficult to determine. Most likely, family members affect one another in a bidirectional and cyclical fashion, in contrast to a unidirectional sphere of influence. In addition, the interactions between numerous and diverse variables is potentially overwhelming to those attempting to understand this process.

It is useful to study parental competence from a systems perspective. The hierarchy of factors influencing the parent-child relationship, both directly and indirectly, must be conceptually organized to provide an understanding of how normal families operate at both a micro and macro level. Such a conceptual model must identify and organize those factors most crucial to our understanding of parenting competence, recognizing the interdependencies between parent, child, and contextual variables. Models of parenting competence offer heuristic benefit to the study of clinical populations by organizing massive amounts of data from normal families into a practical explanation of how families operate successfully or unsuccessfully.

A critical question raised with an ecological or systems perspective is whether processes identified with normal families also function with more extreme forms of family interaction, such as child abuse. To approach this topic, the following section provides an overview of major factors influencing the development of normal parent-child relationships. Because most of the available research is based on nonexperimental and correlational studies, the direction of causation unfortunately cannot be established. Contrasts between desirable and undesirable characteristics of families and individuals within families will be made.

Figure 2.2 indicates the hypothesized directions of influence between different individual, familial, and contextual factors that have been identified in the parenting and child abuse literature (see Belsky, 1984; Bronfenbrenner, 1977; Maccoby & Martin, 1983; Wolfe, 1985a). Parenting style (at the bottom of the figure) has been discussed previously and will be mentioned only briefly here. The remaining factors presented in the figure (parenting history, psychological resources, and social and financial supports) represent aggregate sources of influence on the parent-child relationship that are assumed by the model to operate in an interactive fashion to facilitate or impede successful outcome.

Parenting History

A major premise of an integrated model of the parenting process is that the parent's own history of supportive, positive developmental experiences gives rise to a mature, healthy personality, making him or her more capable of providing sensitive parental care and maximizing child development. *Ipso facto,* parents who lack such experiences are ill-prepared to handle the stresses and responsibilities that are associated with this role. The parents' own developmental history and upbringing is assumed to play an initial role in establishing their psychological well-being and, subsequently, their parental functioning.

Poor parenting practices, such as authoritarian and abusive methods, are believed to be initially acquired in part through modeling and reinforcement of aggression or failure to learn nonaggressive conflict resolution tactics. Burgess and Youngblade (in press) expand upon this basic notion and posit that it is the coercive interactional patterns found among members of dysfunctional and abusive families that are passed on between generations and which account for the continuation of inappropriate parenting behavior by the previously mistreated child. They argue that with consistent exposure to coercive patterns of parent-child or marital interactions, a child has few opportunities to imitate socially skilled adults and to receive differential reinforcement for

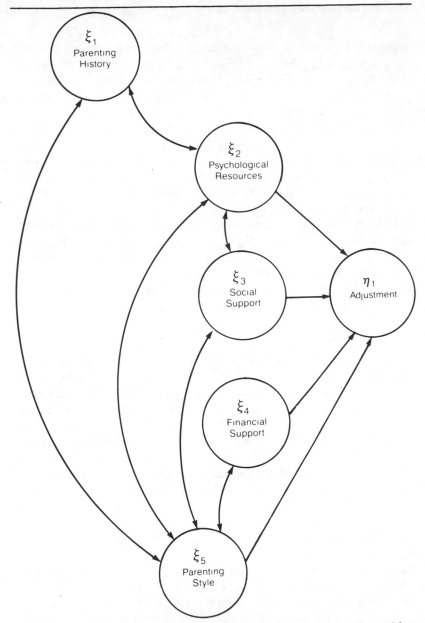

SOURCE: M. R. Gemeinhardt (1986). *A causal modeling approach to parental functioning and children's adjustment.* Unpublished doctoral dissertation, University of Western Ontario. Used with permission.

Figure 2.2 Proposed Model of the Parenting Process

desired behavior. Intergenerational transmission of maladaptive family styles is a central part of social learning explanations of family violence, as discussed in Chapters 3 and 4.

Psychological Resources of the Parent

A consistent picture emerges from prospective and comparative studies of maternal characteristics influencing the parent-child interaction pattern. Mothers who are well-adjusted adults and look forward to their role transition as a parent tend to react positively to their pregnancy and to exhibit interest in and adaptation to their infants when they are born. These expectations about the parenting role appear to be linked to their own family of origin to a large extent, in that healthy childhood experiences lead to positive adulthood adjustment (Maccoby & Martin, 1983).

Brunnquell, Crichton, and Egeland (1981) provide some of the more convincing data arguing for the significance of maternal psychological functioning in the development of the parent-child relationship. Using a prospective, longitudinal design, several important parental characteristics were measured prenatally and at three months. Their sample of 267 "high-risk" mother-infant pairs (that is, mothers selected on the basis of several risk factors for child maltreatment) were divided into Excellent Care and Inadequate Care groups based on subsequent reports of child maltreatment. While they did not find a particular set of parental abilities or attitudes that were clearly associated with child maltreatment at three months, they did find that certain maternal characteristics were related to quality of caretaking. Mothers in the Excellent Care group were found to be of higher intelligence and to express more positive expectations and a better understanding of their parental role than parents in the Inadequate Care group. The researchers discuss the relevance of these findings to child abuse prevention:

> It appears that the mother at risk for abuse or neglect is characterized during pregnancy by a lack of understanding and knowledge concerning parent-child relationships and a negative reaction to pregnancy. After the baby arrives, her anxiety and fear increase in response to the difficulty presented by the baby. She is unable to understand the ambivalence she experiences and responds to her anxiety and fear by becoming more hostile and suspicious. Her increased hostility and suspiciousness interfere further with her ability to relate to the baby and cope with the demands of the situation. (Brunnquell et al., 1981, p. 689).

One mechanism that may explain why well-adjusted parents tend to have well-adjusted offspring is the role that affect plays in bringing past experience to bear on current functioning (see Zajonc, 1980). Studies have shown that when infants and young children repeatedly experience situations in which they are exposed to particular affective states (e.g., happiness, sadness, anger), they acquire similar empathic emotional responses (e.g., Martin, Maccoby, Baron, & Jacklin, 1981). Maccoby and Martin (1983) suggest that classical conditioning processes play a role in developing this pattern. Even if the child is too young to understand the meaning of affective states, parents' feelings of worry, anger, or depression may be communicated to their offspring through associative learning processes. That is, various affective states are associated with a number of early childhood experiences, which are reexperienced at later points in time with similar contextual cues. Thus specific emotional reactions that a child learns early in life may have a chance of enduring throughout the course of child development, and influencing later functioning during adulthood (Maccoby & Martin, 1983).

Although such a hypothesis is extraordinarily difficult to put to empirical test, indirect evidence for its validity can be found from studies of children of parents with major emotional disturbances. Children of manic-depressive parents, for example, are exposed to significant fluctuations in parental affect that appear to have important implications for their affective development. A recent study by Zahn-Waxler, Cummings, McKnew, and Radke-Yarrow (1984) illuminates some of the behavioral and emotional patterns displayed by these children from an early age. Seven male offspring of diagnosed manic-depressive parents from ages 1 to 2½ years served as subjects. In order to study the children's behavior in the context of situations that might pose problems for children of manic-depressive adults, the researchers investigated the interactional styles of these children under a range of circumstances, each conducted with a playmate, a stranger, and their own mother. These circumstances were: (1) handling social interactions in new situations, (2) coping with sudden emotional outbursts, (3) contending with frustration and anxiety due to separation from mother, (4) observing pain and suffering of other persons, and (5) interruption of a pleasurable activity. The children were requested to play in an unfamiliar room amidst either a background of affection and caring, a background of hostility, anger, and rejection (for example, two women returned to the room and had a verbal argument while doing the dishes), a background of reconciliation following the argument, and separation from their mother. To assess how the children dealt with the pain and suffering of others, the child observed an adult bump her leg on a chair and feign injury and pain.

Results indicated that children of manic-depressive parents lacked resilience when faced with frustration or interruptions, had difficulty with give-and-take interpersonal situations, and were prone to react to unpleasant events with aggression (e.g., hitting or grabbing objects from an unfamiliar adult). Following separation from mother, these children were more likely than controls to aggress against their playmates, were more likely to respond to peer aggression with passivity, and displayed more difficulty engaging in friendly play with peers and sharing. In addition to behavior problems, emotional differences were also found. The target children were overly reactive to stressful stimuli, showing heightened upset following adult conflict and difficulty returning to pleasurable activity. The investigators commented that "when exposed to aversive circumstances beyond one's control, emotion may become uncontrolled, behavior inhibited, sadness unresolved, and pleasure difficult. If chronically exposed to similar circumstances in real life, it may become difficult to develop effective coping strategies for dealing with conflict and suffering" (p. 120).

These findings point to a straightforward conclusion: The parent who is well-prepared for the life changes associated with child rearing is less likely to succumb to the increasing stress factors that prevail. This viewpoint, moreover, is very congruent with the principles of preventive mental health—skills, knowledge, and experiences that boost the individual's coping abilities (e.g., their sense of mastery and control over stressful aspects of their role) will increase their resistance to the forces that oppose their healthy adjustment (Dohrenwend, 1978). Such parents are said to be *socially competent* in that they are able to apply interpersonal skills to meet the demands of the situation and provide positive outcomes for the actors involved. To be socially competent in the parenting role, a person must display interpersonal positiveness such as praising, complimenting, or showing affection; the person must be able to observe the demands of a situation in order to choose the appropriate response; and these manifestations must be rewarding to both interactants (Burgess, 1985). The parent who is socially incompetent, on the other hand, fosters incompetence in the child, who in turn reacts aversively to the parent. A vicious cycle of rejection, depression, or low self-esteem may result, leading to child maladjustment and parent-child conflict.

Social and Financial Support

Competent parenting relies not only upon the characteristics of the parent and child but is dependent also upon the context of the parent-child relationship as well (Belsky, 1984). The influence of social supports on an individual's interpersonal behavior and well-being has been of considerable interest to researchers and clinicians working with distressed families. The view that familial stress can be moderated by positive social supports is based on two primary sources of information: (1) early clinical descriptions of abusive parents documenting their isolation from individuals and community resources (e.g., Steele & Pollock, 1968) and their discomfort in interpersonal situations (e.g., Kempe & Helfer, 1972), and (2) the expanding literature on stress and coping, which generally supports the beneficial effect of positive social contacts on psychological well-being and physical health (Mitchell & Trickett, 1980). Sources of support, such as the marital relationship, interactions with coworkers, and the social network are suspected to enhance parental psychological resources (such as self-esteem, knowledge, and self-efficacy), as well as the quality of the parent-child relationship (see Figure 2.2).

Social support appears to enhance parental competence by facilitating problem solving, increasing access to accurate information about children and parenting practices, fostering opportunities for positive reinforcement, and affirming worth in the parenting role (Cutrona, 1984). Although such assistance usually comes from relatives and friends, parents tend to turn secondarily to books for advice when opportunities to consult with knowledgeable persons decline (Clarke-Stewart, 1978).

Financial resources also play a significant role in contributing to the level of crises and turmoil faced by family members. The frequency of familial crises in turn has been linked to the quality of family interactions. For example, Forgatch and Wieder (reported in Patterson, 1982) observed that mothers' reactions to child misbehavior were significantly correlated with the incidence of crises (e.g., car breaking down, quarrels between spouses). Patterson suspects that if a parent responds to a crisis with increased irritability toward the child, effective problem solving is compromised and unsolved problems accumulate and precipitate further crises.

Hetherington, Cox, and Cox (1979) and Wallerstein and Kelly (1981) have observed a similar process of diminished problem solving by parents following divorce. The reestablishment of effective routines between each parent and the child greatly varied, depending upon the availability of social and financial supports to one or both parents. In particular, economic stability, mother's employment, and the development of new intimate relationships by the parents seemed to buffer against adverse effects of new crises. Similar findings have been reported in studies of battered women and their children, in which maternal and child adjustment and recovery from the violence and subsequent turmoil were significantly tied to the availability of social and financial supports, such as housing stability, employment or financial assistance, and counseling resources (Jaffe, Wolfe, Wilson, & Zak, 1986a; Wolfe, Jaffe, Wilson, & Zak, 1985).

At the opposite extreme, social isolation has long been suspected to perpetuate inappropriate child-rearing values and methods (Spinetta & Rigler, 1972). In an early investigation, Young (1964) found that 95% of his severely abusive parents and 83% of his moderately abusive parents had no continuing relationships with others outside the family. The preponderance of such findings in subsequent studies led Garbarino (1977) to propose that isolation from support systems is a *necessary* condition of child maltreatment. According to Garbarino, child abuse is the product of excessive, unmanageable events and the unavailability of potent support systems for the parent that would assist in managing such stress.

An understanding of what produces such isolation and how it affects child rearing is unclear, although several investigators have focused on general deficiencies in social skills combined with multiple sources of stress (Salzinger, Kaplan, & Artemyeff, 1983). It stands to reason that parents who are faced with daily hassles, such as financial difficulties, overcrowding, lack of privacy, underemployment, and crime, have a greater probability of frequent, aversive contacts with others in the community. Under such circumstances, some parents may prefer to isolate themselves as much as possible from unnecessary contacts or involvement with others (Burgess & Youngblade, in press). If we accept that many abusive parents lack the social competence to foster positive relationships, their environmental situation may foster a cycle in which they are more likely to engage in negative exchanges with other community members (e.g., police, employers, neighbors) and further isolate themselves from important parenting resources.

3

THE DEVELOPMENT OF SEVERE PARENT-CHILD CONFLICT AND ABUSE

While recognizing that there is no singular standard of acceptable parenting practices to serve as a benchmark, an understanding of the factors associated with the extreme styles of parenting provides an important beginning to the formulation of a theoretical understanding of child abuse. Throughout the remainder of this book, child abuse will be viewed along the hypothetical continuum that establishes the polar opposites of abusive and healthy parenting styles. From this vantage point, we will look at the factors that influence a parent's movement and position along this continuum. This perspective is in sharp contrast to a view of abusive parents as being "deviant" or distinctly different from other parents. Rather, it raises the supposition that parents who are "predisposed" to difficulties in their role will enter in and out of the "danger zone" that defines the border between acceptable and unacceptable parenting practices.

This chapter first will provide an overview of the major factors associated with the development of healthy versus high-risk parent-child relationships. From this foundation, an abridged review of the major theories of child abuse is presented, followed by a critique and analysis of elements of the theories that are most widely supported by research. A transitional model of child abuse is then formulated to account for parental aggression in terms of the development of the parent-child relationship. This viewpoint is predicated on the notion that maladaptive interaction patterns, like adaptive ones, do not develop simply because of the predilections of the parent or child. To the contrary, they are the result of complex interactions among child characteristics, parental personality and style, the history of the interaction between the child and parent, and the supportive or nonsupportive nature of the broader social context within which the family is embedded (Lamb, 1978). Rather than emphasizing suspected correlates or isolated causes of abuse, the *process* affecting the parent's behavior within the context of the family is the primary focus of attention in the model presented.

FACTORS ASSOCIATED WITH HEALTHY VERSUS HIGH-RISK PARENT-CHILD RELATIONSHIPS

The sequential, interactive nature of the parent-child relationship represents a developmental process that may culminate in different patterns of behavior. Figure 3.1 portrays the distinction between healthy and high-risk outcomes that are a function of previously occurring events. Numerous factors affect these two outcomes, the most salient of which are highlighted below.

Prenatal Factors

Although primarily correlational in nature, a consensus in the medical and social science literature has been formed in support of the critical impact of prenatal factors in establishing the early beginnings of the parent-child relationship. Some of the major highlights of this literature are summarized below (see also Erickson, 1982; Standing Senate Committee on Health, Welfare, & Science, 1980).

Intrauterine care. Serious disturbances in fetal growth and development, as well as later disturbances of the newborn, can be affected prenatally by maternal nutrition, age, substance abuse, and viral and bacterial infections. Such problems are especially problematic among teenaged parents. Mothers' (and perhaps fathers') use of drugs, alcohol, and cigarettes have been linked to infant prematurity, low birth weight, slowed development, and the "difficult child syndrome." These health factors, in addition to genetic endowment, may have a significant impact on the mother's and child's later abilities to establish strong ties.

Maternal adjustment and parental preparation. Although less clearly established than specific teratogenic agents (such as heavy alcohol use or smoking), maternal attitudes and feelings regarding pregnancy are

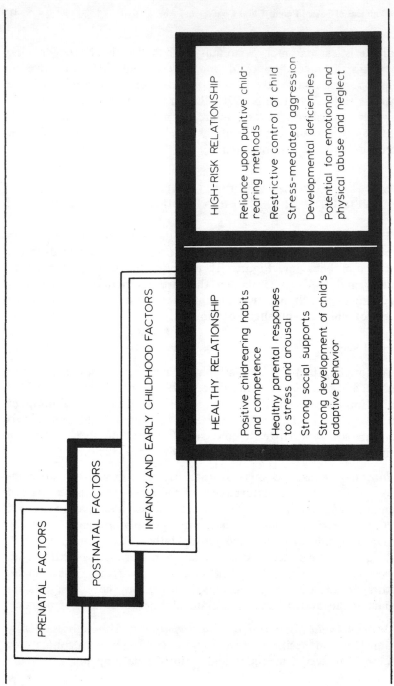

PRENATAL FACTORS

POSTNATAL FACTORS

INFANCY AND EARLY CHILDHOOD FACTORS

HEALTHY RELATIONSHIP

Positive childrearing habits and competence

Healthy parental responses to stress and arousal

Strong social supports

Strong development of child's adaptive behavior

HIGH-RISK RELATIONSHIP

Reliance upon punitive child-rearing methods

Restrictive control of child

Stress-mediated aggression

Developmental deficiencies

Potential for emotional and physical abuse and neglect

Figure 3.1 The Distinction Between Healthy and High-Risk Outcomes

believed to affect complications during pregnancy, labor, and delivery. This is a grave concern among mothers who experience extreme stress or depression during pregnancy, due either to exogenous conditions (such as relationship conflict, violence, or financial instability) or endogenous factors (such as hormonal changes or personality functioning). In addition, how well both parents prepare for their role may predict their degree of success with the newborn. Prospective studies (e.g., Brunnquell et al., 1981; Egeland, Breitenbucher, & Rosenberg, 1980) have shown that high life stress and change during pregnancy are linked to abuse and related problems, especially among mothers who were anxious, unknowledgeable about children, and ill-prepared. The addition of natural caregivers, family members, and similar support opportunities seems to mitigate the effects of life stress and personal adaptation to a significant degree.

Postnatal Factors

During this developmental, interactive sequence we again see precursors to healthy and high-risk parent-child relationships. Most notably, infant-caregiver attachment develops over time through interactional processes that may have a significant effect on the quality of later patterns of care. Parents who were poorly adjusted or prepared before the child's birth are more likely to have negative outcomes with their child, which is somewhat unrelated to the child's birth status (e.g., prematurity, illness, and so on). Furthermore, children who receive poor quality of care during early infancy have been found to show interactional patterns of avoidance or anxious attachment to their caregivers, which leads to further developmental decline (Egeland & Sroufe, 1981).

On the other hand, the parent who is well-prepared for life changes associated with child rearing is less likely to succumb to the increasing stress factors that prevail. Skills, knowledge, experiences, and support that boost the individual's coping abilities will increase their resistance to forces that oppose their healthy adjustment. The same holds true for the infant, whose temperament and responsiveness to his or her caregiver contributes in important ways to the treatment he or she receives.

Infancy and Early Childhood

At this stage of development, parental resources and responses to the child, as well as the child's opportunity and ability to develop adaptive behavior, appear to be critical determinants of the parent-child relationship. Specific qualities that reflect competence in the parenting role, and thereby enhance the parent-child relationship, can be summarized from the child development literature (see Epstein, 1980; Maccoby, 1983; Wolfe, 1985b) as follows:

(1) verbal communication that provides information and intellectual stimulation to the infant;
(2) physical freedom to explore, which allows the infant to develop sensory and motor abilities without undue restriction or control;
(3) responsiveness to the infant's needs in a manner that is consistent with his or her developmental level; and
(4) positive affect that accompanies all supportive verbal and physical interactions.

In essence, if the parent's responses to the young child are age appropriate, peer supported, and otherwise successful from the perspective of the parent's wishes and the child's needs, the risk of relying upon power-assertive control tactics may be reduced, and the child's development of adaptive abilities will be enhanced. As reviewed below, several theoretical perspectives offer reasons some parents and children deviate significantly from this normal developmental process.

THEORETICAL EXPLANATIONS OF ABUSE

Psychopathological Explanations

Since the early 1960s several points of view have had major influences on child abuse theory and research. As graphic descriptions of child abuse trauma began to emerge as a major public and medical concern, the medical profession assumed much of the responsibility for examining the causal factors of abuse, and the social work profession expanded its role as a protection and intervention agent. The cruel and sometimes vicious nature of abusive incidents understandably led researchers and practitioners to search for cognitive, affective, and motivational factors inherent in the individual that could account for such deviant parental behavior. Situational determinants of abuse, such as social isolation, difficult child behavior, and economic disadvantage, were not considered to be as significant in the etiology of the problem, especially since many parents who suffered under similar stress did not harm their children.

The initial clinical portrait of child abusers that emerged from this orientation placed greatest emphasis on the parents' underlying emotional disturbance, and came to be known as the psychopathology, or psychiatric, model (Gelles, 1973; Parke & Collmer, 1975). Clinical descriptions of abusive parents' own childhood experiences attested to the violent or rejecting behavior of their family members. These experiences in turn were linked to the individual's weak personality development and poor self-control. The concept that a fundamental personality disorder is responsible for child abuse was further advanced by reports that abusers often had a propensity for impulsive and/or antisocial acts that extended beyond the parenting role. Abusive behavior was considered to be symptomatic of a character or personality disorder that was characterized by the inability to control aggressive impulses (Spinetta & Rigler, 1972). A parent, according to this explanation, may abuse his or her child due to unmet emotional needs that signify discontentment, anger, or irritability, an inability to balance the child's own needs and capabilities with parental expectations, or emotional scars from their own abusive or deprived family background affecting their ability to care for their own offspring.

Initially, this explanation of child abuse drew support from many fields, in part due to its focus on the psychopathological processes that could account for differences between abusers and nonabusers. Unwittingly, an approach that directed most of the responsibility for abusive behavior squarely on the individual involved was quite acceptable to lawmakers and public interest groups, for this absolved society from blame in contributing to the risk of child abuse (that is, through lack of education, adequate housing and family support programs, employment opportunities, and so on). However, research efforts aimed at distinguishing abusive from nonabusive parents on the basis of personality dimensions (e.g., self-esteem, mood, defense mechanisms, and so on) were largely unsuccessful in supporting the view that abusers suffered from an identifiable form of psychopathology or personality disturbance (Gelles, 1973; Wolfe, 1985a). For example, Gelles (1973) found that of 19 traits reported by researchers to describe abusers, only 3 traits were reported by two or more investigators (these traits were labeled *impulsive, immature,* and *depressed*). More recently, Wolfe (1985a) looked at 19 studies involving abusive parents and matched comparison parents to determine whether relevant distinctions between these populations could be identified. His review concluded that very few studies could differentiate between abusers and nonabusers on the basis of traditional measures of personality disturbance or psychopathology, although abusers were more likely to report stress-related symptoms (such as depression and health problems) that appear to be linked to the parenting role (these symptoms are discussed in Chapter 4).

The lack of consistent findings to support the psychopathological explanation of child abuse does not necessarily condemn its value. The model essentially is an attempt to understand individual characteristics of abusive parents in relation to prior experience and current demands. In so doing it places greater significance on the parent than on any other person or event as the principal cause of the abuse, and relegates situational variables to lesser importance. The absence of evidence supporting the psychopathological viewpoint may be due, in retrospect, to overly broad definitions of personality attributes that were assumed to reflect psychopathology (e.g., thought disorders, affective disorders, character disorders), instead of a more specific focus upon *psychological processes* that could account for behavioral differences, such as coping mechanisms or attributional styles.

Whereas the preponderance of evidence has formed against the view that child-abusive adults are suffering from a major personality defect or mental illness, it is recognized that perhaps as many as 10% of the identified cases do evince such extreme disturbance (Kempe, 1973). We may be witnessing a resurgence of interest in the basic tenets of the psychopathological model, however, as recent investigators wrestle with the problems of defining and measuring individual differences that may help to explain *which* parents abuse their children under *what* situational circumstances (see, for example, Lahey, Conger, Atkeson, & Treiber, 1984; Larrance & Twentyman, 1983; Oldershaw et al., 1986; Salzinger et al., 1983).

Social-Cultural Explanations

Increased interest in the *context* of abusive behavior, such as the nature of family life, environmental stressors affecting the family, and sociodemographic factors, led to a redirection in theoretical perspective at the start of the second decade of child abuse research (Burgess, 1979; Friedman et al., 1981; Gelles, 1973). Proponents of a broader sociocultural viewpoint of family functioning began to criticize the psychopathological explanation by demonstrating the correlational relationship between sociodemographic variables and rates of child abuse (Bronfenbrenner, 1977; Gelles, 1973; Gil, 1970; Light, 1973). This viewpoint, originally referred to as the sociological model and later expanded to become an ecological model of abuse, bases its position on the argument that human behavior should be studied in its own context (Belsky, 1980; Garbarino, 1977). The context of child abuse, it is argued, is described as one of social and economic deprivation, which may be the force that transforms predisposed, high-risk parents into abusive parents (Garbarino & Stocking, 1980). That is, as the social structure in which a parent lives becomes more stressful (or is *perceived* as more stressful), the greater the probability that family violence will surface as an attempt to gain control over irritating, stressful events.

According to this perspective, child abuse is not an isolated social phenomenon or a personality defect of the parent per se—rather, this view maintains that "normal" parents may be socialized into abusive child-care practices through the interaction of cultural, community, and familial influences (see Belsky, 1980; Garbarino & Stocking, 1980; Parke, 1977; Starr, 1979, for an exposition of this process). Cultural sanctioning of violence as an appropriate conflict resolution technique further provides a foundation for the use of corporal punishment in child rearing. If a parent was frequently exposed to harsh physical punishment as a child, he or she may have a greater propensity toward viewing such behavior as normative, and inhibitions against physical force may be lessened (Bandura, 1973; Maurer, 1974).

Socialization practices that can lead to child abuse may flourish in an atmosphere where the "costs" of being violent are expected to be less than the "rewards" obtained through such means (Gelles, 1983). For example, when effective social controls over family relations are not present (such as police laying charges against perpetrators of domestic violence; Jaffe, Wolfe, Telford, & Austin, 1986), such behavior is implicitly condoned. Gelles and Straus (1979) further emphasize the lack of rewards for nonviolent methods of child control. According to this exchange/social control theory, under stressful circumstances a high-risk parent (one who is predisposed to violence due to their own learning history or coping abilities) may feel that he or she is expending a great deal of time and energy with little positive reinforcement from the child. The parent may feel resentment toward the child, thus lowering inhibitions toward excessive physical punishment. It follows from this viewpoint that abusive practices are not so much a function of individual behavior as much as they are a function of social and cultural forces *that establish the parameters of individual behavior.*

Some proponents of the social-cultural viewpoint argue that factors associated with poverty and inadequate physical resources form the single most influential cause of child abuse (Gil, 1970; Pelton, 1978). This point was highlighted in a major study in Pennsylvania, where Garbarino (1976) found that socioeconomic factors accounted for 36% of the variance in rates of child abuse. No other factor, singly or in combination with similar variables, has been shown to account for such a significant proportion of variance in child abuse reports. Unemployment, restricted educational and occupational opportunities, and unstable and/or violent family situations also have been found to be major correlates of child abuse, and these findings are often cited in support of social-cultural explanations of this phenomenon.

To counterbalance the significance of these social-cultural forces, it should be recognized that socioeconomic factors offer only limited predictive or preventive value regarding aversive parent-child relationships (Brown & Harris, 1978; Garmezy, 1983). A more specific understanding is needed of the *processes* responsible for the relatively small percentage of adults exposed to these environmental hardships who eventually exhibit abusive behavior. The third theoretical perspective, described below, aligns the social context of abuse with suspected psychological processes that may account for individual differences in responding to the demands of child rearing.

Social-Interactional Explanations

The important psychological variables that mediate between environmental pressures and an abusive episode warrant further theoretical integration. Clearly, many parents can operate under a barrage of stressful stimuli without unleashing anger or abuse toward their offspring; likewise, many parents use corporal punishment with their children without causing injury or escalating to an unbridled attack. While the psychopathological and social-cultural models provided ample coverage of the potential factors that may influence an individual's aggressive behavior, they have fallen short in explicating the psychological processes that explain why some parents become abusive toward their offspring and others do not.

The social interactional model (Burgess, 1979; Parke & Collmer, 1975) attempts to bridge this gap by focusing on the interactional *process* between parent and child, within both the familial context and the larger social structure. These processes resemble those occurring in normal and clinically distressed parent-child relationships, such as reciprocation of aversive behavior, reinforcement of inappropriate behavior, ineffective use of punishment, conditioned emotional arousal, and stable, internal, and global attributions for child misbehavior. Drawn largely from clinical and developmental research on parent-child interactions, this viewpoint approaches the etiology and exacerbation of abuse in terms of the dynamic interplay between individual, family, and social factors, in relation to both past (e.g., exposure to abuse as a child) and present (e.g., a demanding child) events. The parent's learning history, interpersonal experiences, and intrinsic capabilities are regarded as predisposing characteristics presumed to be important contributors to an abusive episode or pattern (Friedman et al., 1981).

Although social-interactional theorists are concerned primarily with the current behavior of the abusive parent in the context of the family or community, psychological mechanisms such as perceptions, interpretations of events, and affective expression are recognized as important mediators in influencing parent-child interactions (LaRose & Wolfe, in press). Thus interactional processes are not necessarily limited to observable behaviors, such as parental criticisms, child behavior problems, yelling, or displays of anger, but include cognitive and affective processes (e.g., intelligence, attitudes, attributions for behavior) that may mediate behavioral exchanges.

Learning-based explanations of aggressive behavior also form an expanding portion of the social-interactional approach to child abuse. This is because most incidents of child abuse involve a great deal more than the use of corporal punishment with a child. The potential for injury to the child dramatically increases as the parent begins to lose control of his or her actions and accelerates from low- to high-intensity punitive behavior (Vasta, 1982). This transition from anger to aggression is viewed as a key factor in explaining other forms of interpersonal violence (Berkowitz, 1974), and has been receiving wider attention among child abuse researchers (e.g., Frodi & Lamb, 1980; Vasta & Copitch, 1981). In response to difficult child behavior and a stress-filled environment, therefore, a parent may experience conditioned negative arousal (feelings of tension, anger, or rage) and/or negative attributions ("my kid is doing this on purpose to upset me") that serve to mediate an aggressive retaliation.

The social interactional model and its corollaries have had a pronounced influence on research productivity in child abuse over the past decade. Such research has taken many forms, with different investigators approaching the problem by studying behavioral, cognitive, and affective derivatives of child abuse. By and large these studies have included observations of parent-child interactions in the home and clinic, analog experiments of conditions that favor abusive interactions, psychophysiological studies of parental arousal to child stimuli, self-report of parental attributions for child misconduct, and treatment outcome studies that focus on changing critical aspects of the interactional process that may lead to abuse.

Parents who abuse their children, according to this analysis, should display rates and patterns of aversive behaviors that distinguish them from nonabusers. In return, other family members, especially the abused child, are viewed as active participants in the escalation of anger and aggression. Empirical support for this explanation of child abuse has been progressively strong, especially among the interactional studies that have documented the type and degree of negative interaction patterns between abusive family members. For example, comparative studies of family interaction have indicated that abusers display reciprocal patterns of behavior with their children and spouses that are proportionately more aversive and less prosocial than nonabusers (Wolfe, 1985a). A number of questions remain, however, regarding how psychological processes (e.g., operant and respondent conditioning, cognitive attributions) modulate parental aggression toward a child.

A Theoretical Commentary

The distinctions between the above theoretical formulations of child abuse have become less clear in recent years, which may reflect the fact that they share important commonalities and do not necessarily represent radically opposed viewpoints of abusive parents. All three models reflect attempts to understand individual characteristics of abusive parents in relation to prior experience and current demands. The major distinction that can be inferred between these explanations is the amount of significance each places on the parent as the principal cause of maltreatment, as opposed to situational circumstances or the larger sociocultural milieu.

The two distinctive key elements that appear repeatedly among theoretical explanations of child abuse are the social interactional processes among family members and the frustration-aggression relationship (Gelles & Straus, 1979). These two theoretical dimensions together provide ample coverage of the known findings regarding child abuse and interpersonal aggression, with the possible oversight of attributional explanations (see Averill, 1983; Zillman, 1979; discussion to follow). Neither component is static or assumed to be inherent in the individual or family. Rather, social interactional and aggression processes are useful in explaining the constant changes in the behavior of family members in response to events within or outside of the family unit.

Child abuse theories often imply that the "cause" of abuse resides in the person, situation, or the social context. Yet this intuitively appealing conclusion runs counter to reports by many nonabusive parents who openly admit that they sometimes feel an "urge" to strike their child when angry or upset. Available research findings indicate that the cause of abuse is not related to any lack of a particular resource, exposure to any particular pathogenic process, mental illness, or "stress." More accurately, child abuse can best be explained as the *result of an interaction* between the parent and child within a system that seldom provides alternative solutions (e.g., through exposure to appropriate parental models, education, and supports), or clear-cut restraints (e.g., laws, sanctions, and consequences) for the use of excessive force to resolve common child-rearing conflicts.

The theories also expound upon the importance of the social structure within which the family is functioning. That is, a supportive and educational social structure has a strong impact in guiding parents' development of positive child-rearing patterns. The drastic change in social structure that has occurred over the past generation may be creating confusion and rebellion on the part of some parents, however. Some families have not yet adapted to the changes in societal expectations and tolerance vis-à-vis child-rearing norms, especially regarding the use of corporal punishment. For example, marks left by the use of an object to spank a child are a very common source of evidence in child abuse reports. This state of affairs suggests that at least some proportion of the population is unaware of the risks of using objects to punish children, or alternatively refuses to view such behavior as a "risk." Although there is often a large degree of erosion in socialization practices between a parent's family of origin and present cultural norms (Maccoby & Martin, 1983), such changes may leave a gap in child-rearing knowledge and ability among parents who are slow or resistant to learn unfamiliar techniques.

In view of the above, one cause of child abuse can be attributed to ignorance—not only on the part of the parent regarding child-rearing methods and expectations, but also on the part of other family members, community agents, and the broader social system. Information regarding appropriate-child rearing methods and norms often is not emphasized or made available unless a parent either is highly self-motivated to pursue the information, or he or she deviates considerably from expectations. This lack of information partially may explain why so many reported child abusers are of lower-income and lower-status backgrounds, less educated, more isolated, and so forth— they may not know, or fail to attempt, to seek assistance or guidance in their parenting role, and it is seldom available to them unless ordered by the court. Overcoming resistance on the part of parents as well as community agents to the provision of widely available parenting support services at present poses a major challenge to community-based child abuse prevention approaches.

EFFECTS OF STRESS
ON THE FAMILY SYSTEM

"Stress" has received a major portion of blame for serving as the catalyst that turns an unpleasant situation into an abusive one. Theories cannot fully explain the child abuse phenomenon without the addition of the concept of stress that gives rise to maladaptive coping responses, since abusive parents are clearly not violent under all circumstances. What seems to be responsible for aggravating the level of conflict between family members is not any particular type of stress, but rather the presence of a stress-filled environment that may originate from a number of sources (e.g., poor adaptive abilities; socioeconomic disadvantage).

The Relation Between Stress,
Family Conflict, and Child Development

There is some degree of unavoidable confusion on the part of investigators interested in clarifying the nature of stress and its relationship to family conflict and child development. A single stressor, such as sudden financial pressures, that may have triggered an abusive episode is not typically sufficient to account for the development of maladaptive behavior among abused children, for example. In most cases, stress can best be described as a disequilibrating event that temporarily disturbs the functioning of family member(s) and initiates a chain of adaptive or maladaptive responses.

Kagan (1983) has criticized prior efforts to define stress in relation to child development and family functioning on the basis of their failure to consider the psychological processes that may alter the impact of a stressor. Instead, many definitions of stress are based on the association between certain conditions (that is, stressors) and socially undesirable outcomes (for example, health problems or emotional disorders). For example, harsh punishment, frequent change of residence, divorce, poverty, or parents who are indifferent are classified as stressful (by most standard definitions) because we believe that they create emotional reactions on the part of the recipient, and because these conditions are predictive of poor outcome reactions. A problem with this approach is that it ignores the interaction between the event and the attributes of the individual. Although this common method of defining stress may be useful during initial stages of inquiry, it can be misleading because the outcome does not always follow from the events. Kagan explains this outdated viewpoint of stress with the metaphor of a hammer blow that creates a uniform deformation in the homogeneous surface that it strikes. To the contrary, the impact of any stressor depends to a large extent upon the characteristics of the individual who must cope with the stressor.

The above clarification of what constitutes "stress" has important implications for conceptualizing the relationship between uncontrollable events ("stress") and family conflict. First of all, there may not be a simple linear relationship between the *amount and type of stress* and the *degree of violence* between family members. Rather than having a direct influence, the presence of stressful stimuli may affect the "timing" or contingent relationship between a parent and child. This was demonstrated in a study by Dumas and Wahler (1985), in which mothers who were repeatedly subjected to high rates of adverse setting events (for instance, noisy neighbors, conflict with relatives, and so on) were found to be inconsistent in matching their disciplinary actions to the behavior of their children. Such inconsistency was not found among those mothers who were not barraged by stressful events. Furthermore, we must avoid the tendency to assume that child abuse is a form of stress to the child that leads to a uniformly negative outcome. It is more cautious to say that the impact depends on such factors as the child's age, prior interactions with the parent, and his or her interpretations of the parental act (see Chapter 5). Thus stress may appear in many different forms for different individuals, and can best be understood as any events or demands that create an acute or chronic imbalance for the individual or the family system. This imbalance in turn is typically met by counterpressure from the individual's coping efforts to return himself or herself to a more comfortable state of equilibrium.

A common theme reemerges among studies of stress and child development: The negative or positive impact of a stressful event or events depends to a large extent upon (1) the degree of interruption and disarray that may be set into action by the original event and (2) the presence of psychological and physical "buffers" that regulate the harshness of the stressor in tangible and intangible ways. This relationship has been most readily observed in studies of children who have undergone acute forms of stress. For example, children who are hospitalized for medical reasons, as well as children who experience the birth of a younger sibling, typically display what could be termed a "stress reaction" (exhibiting more tearful episodes, sleep disturbances, bed-wetting), yet such events seldom lead to long-term problems without the presence or absence of other factors. Most notably, children may be as much affected by parental attitudes and mental state as by any stressful hospital procedures or changes in the family (see Rutter, 1983). This is supported by findings indicating that persisting disturbance of the child is more likely if the child comes from a deprived or disturbed family, or if the previous parent-child relationship was poor (Quinton & Rutter, 1976). Adverse effects from stress seem to potentiate one another so that the combined effects of two stressors together are greater than the sum of the two separately.

Children of divorce. Parental divorce represents a major stress on the child, and its impact on the child's behavioral and emotional adjustment has been documented (Hetherington et al., 1979; Wallerstein & Kelly, 1981). Following divorce, children (especially boys) are apt to show a rather sudden increase in behavior problems, such as having tantrums, noncompliance, and refusing to go to school. The suspected reasons for this reaction are similar to those noted above: In the aftermath of divorce, both parents tend to be inconsistent, less affectionate, and lacking in control of their children. During the first year following separation or divorce, mothers have been described as more depressed, self-involved, erratic, less supportive, and ineffectual, and fathers have been found initially to be unduly permissive and indulgent, and then to increase their amount of restrictiveness and negative sanctions (Rutter, 1983). These changes in parenting behavior may serve to increase the degree of stress on the child that already has been set in motion by parental separation. Furthermore, when parental conflict and discord continues to pervade beyond the separation, this conflict is believed to contribute most significantly to the negative, traumatic impact of parental separation and divorce on the child (Emery, 1982).

Children of battered women. Children who have heard or seen their fathers abusing their mothers have undergone very stressful and frightening experiences. An understanding of their adaptation and adjustment following such events lends additional insight into the plight of abused children and their family processes. Children who have been brought to battered women's shelters by their mothers following episodes of marital violence have been reported as showing elevated emotional and behavioral problems. In one study of 102 school-aged children who had witnessed marital violence and 96 comparison children who had not, 33% of the boys and 20% of the girls who were exposed to violence were found to be within the range of clinically distressed children (Wolfe et al., 1985). Boys were displaying both internalizing (e.g., frequent crying, sadness, peer withdrawal) and externalizing problems (e.g., aggression, noncompliance) that were usually quite noticeable to adults. Girls, on the other hand, were reported to show fewer overt, behavioral signs of distress than boys, although subtle changes in their peer relationships and school performance were reported by parents and teachers (Jaffe, Wolfe, Wilson, & Zak, 1986b). Although observing parental conflict and violence is certainly a major source of stress on these children's lives, the latter study found that the impact that such experiences has on the children was mediated by other family processes. Most notably, the mother's emotional adjustment and the degree of family instability and disadvantage to which the child has also been exposed (e.g., school changes, drop in financial resources, repeated marital separations) were strong predictors of the extent of behavioral disturbance displayed by the child.

Relating these findings with children of divorce and family violence back to the original theme of how stressful events affect family functioning and children's adjustment helps to clarify the somewhat indirect manner in which the child is affected by adverse family conditions. Studies of parental conflict and wife abuse provide us with examples of how the child's daily routine and relationships with family members can be disturbed, which further sets into motion a chain of debilitating or supportive actions that mediate the impact on the child. In essence, the stressful quality of these major events lies in their effects on patterns of family interactions and relationships, which then serve to interfere with the child's social environment. The immediate stress associated with a critical life event may play a far lesser role in making such events significant hazards to development than do changes and stressors in the child's social environment associated with the event (e.g., parental adjustment problems following divorce or conflict; disruptions in school placement and peer relationships). Shifts in conditions of the child's environment as a function of family stress factors, therefore, may be the process that is most "stressful" to the child, pointing again to the importance of considering the child's innate or acquired ability to adapt to change.

A TRANSITIONAL MODEL OF CHILD ABUSE

The theoretical viewpoints discussed in the beginning of this chapter offer a number of explanations as to *why* a parent might abuse a child. As evidence, proponents of each model cite various studies that have demonstrated a relationship between abuse and theoretically relevant variables, such as personality dimensions, sociodemographic conditions, and behavioral interactions between abusive parents and their children. Each approach has contributed new knowledge to our understanding of child abuse, yet further integration of the findings into a transitional model is needed to address the concern of *how* parents gradually acquire the preconditions that seem to lead to the rather sudden onset of abusive behavior.

Several changes and additions to current explanations of child abuse emerge from the following model, which places an emphasis on the *development* of abusive behavior within the family context. Rather than focusing on observable factors that are often present once a family has been labeled or reported as abusive (such as their demographic, personality, and family characteristics), this viewpoint looks at the process by which several identified contributors to child abuse become transformed over time into a high-risk or abusive situation. This approach to studying social phenomena is certainly not revolutionary or unique; in fact, it leans heavily upon the fundamental views of the social-interactional model of abuse and family aggression (that child abuse is the result of an interactional process involving the parent, child, and contextual variables). The current discussion, however, takes into greater account the importance of the process that changes aspects of the parent-child relationship gradually over time into more aversive and high-risk interactions. As well, the influence of health-promoting, compensatory factors that may serve to reduce or alter the gradual development of abusive patterns are drawn into this analysis.

The current transitional model of abuse is based on two presuppositions. First, the development of abusive child-rearing patterns is presumed to follow a somewhat predictable course in the absence of intervention or major compensatory factors. In the following discussion this course will be described in reference to stages, which serve to underscore the contention that child abuse develops from a gradual transformation in the parent-child relationship from mild to very harmful interactions. Accordingly, the initial stage of the development of abusive behavior is *relatively benign* in comparison to later stages, in that the parent has not as yet behaved in a manner that significantly interferes with the parent-child relationship. However, failure to deal effectively with the demands of their role early on (both within and outside of the family context) can readily lead to increased pressure on the parent-child relationship and a concomitant increase in the probability of aggressive behavior. This process therefore bears some resemblance to other forms of problem behavior that develop over time as a result of ineffective or inappropriate responses to stressful or commonplace demands (e.g., drug and alcohol abuse).

The second presupposition required of this model relates to the importance of psychological processes that are linked to the expression of anger, arousal, and coping reactions in adults. These processes are held to be responsible for determining the positive or negative outcome at each successive stage in the development of the parent-child relationship. Specifically, they include operant and respondent learning principles for the acquisition and maintenance of behavior, cognitive-attributional processes that influence an individual's perception and reaction to stressful events, and emotional conditioning processes that determine the individual's degree of physiological arousal, perceived discomfort, and self-control under stressful circumstances.

These psychological processes, singly or in combination, may accentuate or attenuate the impact of any of the major factors associated with child abuse. A parent who is reinforced (by the cessation of aversive child behavior) for using harsh physical punishment, for example, may continue to emit such behavior under similar circumstances, even in the absence of many of the additional high-risk factors. At the other extreme, a parent who is inundated with highly stressful demands (e.g., living in low-income housing, several difficult children in the home, nonsupportive relatives) could, according to this process model, escape from the pitfalls that lead to abusive behavior if he or she has learned very effective coping responses that serve to protect against the aversive impact of these events, such as positive child management skills, relaxation and distraction techniques, and problem-focused coping that serve to reduce arousal and perceived stress. Therefore, different outcomes to child abuse risk factors are clearly possible when the psychological resources of the individual and the family are taken into consideration, which is the premise for psychologically based interventions.

The course of the development of abusive behavior has been conceptualized by stages in Figure 3.2. This figure provides an overview of the destabilizing and compensatory factors that will be part of the following discussion. The course initially begins with the parent's own preparation (in terms of psychological and social resources, modeling, and similar learning experiences from childhood) and current style of coping with the daily competing demands of their role as a parent. Problems in these areas may then lead to poor management of acute crises and provocation that heighten parental anger, arousal, and level of discomfort. When this point is reached (which may occur early in the development of the parent-child relationship or after a long period of reasonable stability), the parent may become easily overwhelmed by the amount and intensity of uncontrollable events impinging upon him or her. The child's behavior or characteristics serve as the "triggering event" that unleashes a floodgate of anger and frustration that leads to abuse; (persons or things other than the child may likewise trigger an episode of anger and aggression, such as a coworker, spouse, neighbor, household pet, and so on). Finally, a habitual pattern of irritability, arousal, and/or avoidance of responsibility may become established, which serves to perpetuate the use of power-assertive or uninvolved child-rearing methods.

Stage I: Reduced Tolerance for Stress and Disinhibition of Aggression

What factors initially play a role in setting into motion a malignant cycle of parent-child relations? Because it is unlikely that child abuse suddenly erupts from a placid family environment, we need to look at the processes that are suspected to remove the parent's inhibition to use excessive force against a child.

First of all, we must consider the manner in which such inhibition of aggression is initially established. If one assumes that the *capability* of using aggressive or coercive behavior is innate, its individual expression is most likely regulated to a certain extent by environmental forces (see

| DESTABILIZING FACTORS | COMPENSATORY FACTORS |

STAGE I:
Reduced Tolerance for Stress and Disinhibition of Aggression

- Weak preparation for parenting
- Low control, feedback, predictability
- Stressful life events

- Supportive spouse
- Socioeconomic stability
- Success at work, school
- Social supports and models

STAGE II:
Poor Management of Acute Crises and Provocation

- Conditioned emotional arousal
- Sources of anger and aggression
- Appraisal of harm/loss; threat

- Improvement in child behavior
- Community programs for parents
- Coping resources

STAGE III:
Habitual Patterns of Arousal and Aggression with Family Members

- Child's habituation to physical punishment
- Parent's reinforcement for using strict control techniques
- Child's increase in problem behavior

- Parental dissatisfaction with physical punishment
- Child responds favorably to noncoercive methods
- Community restraints/services

Figure 3.2: A Transitional Model of Child Abuse

Bandura, 1973). Accordingly, appropriate inhibition typically evolves throughout childhood and early adulthood as the individual learns to discriminate between aggressive and assertive behavior, to develop self-control abilities, and to use prosocial means of attaining his or her goals. Because these counteraggressive abilities are learned in large part through family interactions, it stands to reason that the family of origin is a prime suspect in the initial failure to establish inhibitory controls for aggressive behavior. This is supported, of course, by the child abuse literature that typifies the abuser's family of origin as a training ground for interpersonal violence and/or lowered social competence. This training is inadvertently accomplished through the well-known principles of learning and social cognition, that is, modeling of aggressive problem-solving tactics via marital violence and corporal punishment, rehearsal and reinforcement (or lack of effective punishment) of aggressive behavior with siblings and peers, the absence of opportunities to learn appropriate problem-resolution approaches, and the establishment of a cognitive viewpoint that adheres to strict family roles and low self-efficacy. All of these processes have been linked to the disinhibition, or increased expression, of aggressive behavior in populations other than abusive parents (Bandura, 1973; Patterson, 1982; Zillman, 1979).

The above learning experiences throughout childhood and early adulthood increase the likelihood of creating a *predisposition* toward aggressive behavior under circumstances that resemble the original conditions in some fashion (e.g., similar affective arousal or behavioral goals were witnessed or directly experienced at an earlier period). But what factors now play a critical role in mediating the expression of aggressive behavior once the individual becomes a parent? The current model maintains that the response to noxious events can be markedly altered by psychological factors. This is essentially stating that the parent's response to the child is a function of the interaction between level of external stress and level of internal tolerance/coping. If stress is low and/or tolerance is high (e.g., when the child is playing quietly in a manner that pleases the parent and the parent has had an "easy day") the parent's response may be quite acceptable. When reversed (e.g., the child is demanding to watch television and the parent is very tired and wants to be left alone), inhibition of anger and aggression may be weakened.

Levine (1983) identifies three psychological factors that have been most consistently linked to adult responses to stressful events: (1) control, or the ability to make coping responses during stress; (2) the amount of feedback or information one receives following an aversive event or the response to that event; and (3) the degree of predictability one has of the stressor. Control is often considered to be the most important psychological factor mediating the impact of stress (Lefcourt, 1973), for it allows the individual to avoid or escape the undesired event. As Levine sums up this relationship, "having control is helpful, losing control is aversive, and previous experience with control can significantly alter the ability to cope with subsequent aversive stimuli" (1983, p. 115). Feedback also serves a facilitative function in managing stress since it conveys to the individual whether he or she has done the right thing and whether or not it has been effective. Predictability, on the other hand, is less clear-cut but seems to be related to the individual's *sense* of control;

that is, an event may be *perceived* as less stressful if one believes that he or she can exercise personal choice, which is predicted on the basis of prior experience.

What implications does this knowledge have for an understanding of child abuse in its early stages? First of all, it is important to restate the significance of the parent's ability to cope with fluctuating levels of stress. Successful coping sets the stage for a more successful parent-child relationship, whereas coping failure early on sets in motion further debilitation of the relationship. We know from related research with other adult-clinical populations that stressful life events play a significant role in provoking the onset of suicide, depression, neurotic disorders, and health-related disorders (Brown & Harris, 1978). The common, everyday problems related to marriage, work, and personal accomplishment or rejection seem to have a greater influence on behavior in the long term than the major crises, such as severe illness or financial ruin (Rutter, 1983). Thus it is reasonable to assume that a similar process may be operative in the establishment of abusive patterns of interaction—stressful life events may provoke abusive or neglectful responses on the part of parents who are predisposed to such behavior through prior learning experiences. In addition, the three factors noted in the previous paragraph can also influence the expression of aggressive behavior in persons who are predisposed to such behavior. In fact, the use of power-assertive or aggressive tactics with family members may be easily viewed as a successful, albeit inappropriate, method of attaining control, feedback, and predictability on the part of the user, thus establishing a persistent pattern of coercion.

Stage II: Poor Management of Acute Crises and Provocation

Stage II represents the hypothetical point in the development of abusive behavior in which the parent's previous attempts or methods of managing life stress and child behavior begin to fail significantly in their effectiveness. During the previous stage (which some parents may continue with indefinitely while others pass through rapidly), the parent has often acquired his or her own style of "coping" or dealing with the mounting stresses that accompany their role. Typically, these methods involve short-term and self-defeating solutions to their problems, such as excessive alcohol or drug usage, frequent relocations (for employment, to escape debtors, and so forth), harsh punishment of the children, palliative medications, and so forth. Once the parent has reached the point where he or she begins to recognize the futility or ineffectiveness of his or her efforts, a major issue becomes the real or imagined *threat* to their remaining control (over the child, other family members, and related aspects of life). Negative feedback and poor control and predictability of child-rearing and family matters all serve to exacerbate feelings of "losing control" (a term that many abusive parents use to describe their feelings prior to the abusive episode).

It is at this juncture that the risk of child abuse begins to redouble. In the face of mounting stress and pressure that has not been previously dealt with effectively, the parent may at first conclude that he or she needs to "step up" the intensity of the punishment and power assertion that is showing signs of weakness and failure. This "decision" to increase punishment or aversive control can be described more precisely as a split-second response to perceived threat and provocation that has not been attenuated by other intrinsic or extrinsic feedback. In other words, the parent's behavior is momentarily irrational in respect to its intention, excessiveness, and expression.

Two psychological processes are particularly relevant to our understanding of this escalation from punishment to abuse: the effects of mood states and emotional arousal (e.g., increased sensitivity to stimuli, agitation) and the parent's perceptions of areas of stress related to the parenting role (e.g., perceived loss of control, placement of blame for feelings of discomfort), which both serve a radical function in the disinhibition of aggression. The following section will explicate the role of these processes in relation to the parent's response to the child's behavior.

The effects of mood states and arousal on the expression of aggressive behavior. One of the baffling questions that arises in attempts to comprehend abusive behavior is how the child can provoke such a gross overreaction from his or her own parent or, conversely, why it is that the child receives the brunt of the parent's anger and rage? Social-psychological studies regarding the primacy of mood or affect on behavioral responses and studies on the development and expression of aggressive behavior offer some insight into this relationship.

It is not surprising to find that an individual's behavior can be greatly influenced by his or her mood. Laboratory studies of this relationship have shown that when a positive mood is artificially induced, for example, people are better able to postpone gratification and are more willing to comply with the requests of others (see Maccoby, 1983). But what is even more salient to the study of child abuse is the discovery that experiences can have affective "tags" when stored in memory. When these experiences are recalled at some later point in time, therefore, the recollection of the actual event is biased by the person's mood at the time of the event. In a similar manner, if a person's current mood is one of sadness or depression, he or she is more likely to recall other previously sad or depressing events (Bower, 1981).

It may be deduced from the above discussion that the behavior of abusive parents is affected by the association between the child's current problem behavior and similar circumstances from previous stressful encounters. The parent's previous mood of distress and anger toward the child is recalled by the child's current behavior or expression, leading to an overgeneralized (more angry, more aggressive) response by the parent. In effect, the parent's affective state at the time of an aversive encounter with the child is *classically conditioned* to particular aspects of the child's behavior and/or appearance (e.g., voice tone, facial expression, crying). When these child cues are again present, the conditioned emotional response (of anger, irritation, rage, or other feelings that were previously elicited) quickly reappears and contributes to the parent's inability to maintain self-control and rational thought. Presumably, the adult is responding to cues that have been previously associated with frustration or anger, and the adult's behavior toward the child may be potentiated by these conditioning experiences (Berkowitz, 1983; Vasta, 1982).

Part of the answer to why a child may become the victim of unmitigated anger and aggression from the parent also comes from experiments with normal subjects. These studies have determined that anger (a precursor of aggression) is a highly interpersonal emotion that typically involves a close affectional relationship betweeen the angry person and the target (Averill, 1983). The person's level of arousal and his or her beliefs about the *source* of arousal play a critical role in determining the actual expression of aggression. A person may become aroused (e.g., hyperalert, tense, anxious, in a state of high emotion) by a number of sources, such as frustration, extraneous physical arousal (e.g., exercise, exertion), or aggressive stimuli (e.g., arguing with a neighbor). If the person is provoked by someone or something following arousal from one of the above sources, aggression is more likely *if the person is unaware of the source of the extraneous arousal and misattributes it to the current provocation* (that is, the child). This process has been termed "transfer of arousal" (Averill, 1983), and may account for episodes of abuse that occur in response to mild provocation from the child or spouse. That is, the abusive parent may have been angered and aroused by a previous encounter (with an employer, neighbor, or motorist), which lowers his or her threshold for anger and aggression with family members.

In brief, a person must believe he or she has a reason to be angry, or to have some form of justification for anger. Averill (1983) maintains that a vicious cycle is formed between anger and aggression: Feelings of anger (which may have derived from a number of different sources) create a need for justification. Once the anger is justified (e.g., blaming the child for causing the parent to feel angry, upset, and hassled), this justification in return encourages further anger and aggression. Vasta (1982) argues that this negative arousal interferes with rational problem solving such that with an increase in arousal, the parent's awareness of the outcome of his or her actions diminishes and the disciplinary behaviors come under control of emotional and reflexive factors. In this state, the physical punishment may be prolonged and the act itself can become invigorating or cathartic. Arousal is reduced only if the "attack" is continued to the point of exhaustion (Zillman, 1979). Factors that influence the parent's level of anger and arousal, furthermore, may have a cumulative and multiplicative effect over time, thus underscoring their importance in preventing the recurrence of abuse.

Perceptions of areas of stress related to the parenting role. How a parent views of child-rearing situations or evaluates and copes with life changes has been found to relate to how effective or adaptive that parent is in promoting child compliance and development (Kaplan, Eichler, & Winickoff, 1980). For this reason, the evaluative processes a parent goes through to conclude that the interaction with his or her child is stressful or nonstressful merit consideration.

The transactional model of stress (Folkman, 1984; Lazarus, 1981) describes a twofold process by which a person evaluates a situation as stressful. First, the person evaluates a specific transaction with respect to his or her own welfare (e.g., their happiness, contentment, prosperity), and second, he or she evaluates coping resources and options. Stressful appraisals are those where the outcome is viewed as a harm/loss, a threat, or a challenge. Appraisals of harm/loss or threat are characterized by negative emotions, whereas a challenge is characterized by pleasurable emotions, such as excitement and eagerness. A crucial factor that accounts for these distinct outcomes appears to be the degree of control an individual believes he or she has over the situation—events that are seen as being out of the person's control are perceived as harmful or threatening, whereas others that are viewed as being within the person's control are challenging.

This model has apparent value in understanding the cognitive processes affecting the likelihood of child abuse. During Stage II of the development of abusive behavior, the parent begins to view familiar, difficult interactions with the child as being "out of control" and as a deliberate attempt to defy the parent's authority (Feshbach, 1980). We know from research on aggression that acts that are perceived as deliberate evoke significantly more aggression than behaviors appraised as accidental (e.g., Shantz & Voyandoff, 1973). Even if the child is relatively compliant and well mannered, the abusive parent may view other aspects of the environment as highly demanding and therefore unjust. As a consequence, when the child cries or fusses to seek attention or assistance, the parent may appraise the situation in such a way that leads to a conclusion of provocation by the child (LaRose & Wolfe, 1987). As stated earlier, such an appraisal can lead to justification for using excessive physical punishment to gain control over at least some aspect of a stressful and unsatisfactory situation.

Stage III: Habitual Patterns of Arousal and Aggression with Family Members

Some incidents of child abuse are relatively isolated, one-time episodes that have few of the historical and contemporaneous "warning signs" that have been discussed in this book. However, these incidents are much less common than the "typical" pattern of abuse, in which reports of maltreatment surface after a history of difficult parent-child relations, strained family relationships, and chronic levels of stress and inadequate resources. It is these latter, more typical circumstances that are the focus of our concern during Stage III in the development of abusive behavior.

The current transitional model views Stage II as the point where stressful circumstances culminate into abusive or high-risk practices. But the process certainly does not end once the parent has begun to fail in his or her attempt to manage the child or react to stress with physically coercive methods. Stage III represents the repetition of provocative stimuli (e.g., child behavior problems, frustration, arousal, etc.) and the escalation of the parent's response to such stimuli in terms of intensity, frequency, and duration. Occasional stressful events (such as during Stage II) now become commonplace, and the adult's ability to adapt to the onslaught of constant disruption and negative events becomes more greatly impaired. A habitual pattern of stress, arousal, and overgeneralized responses to the child and other significant persons becomes entrenched, often despite the parent's self-perception that he or she is doing everything within his or her power to reverse this process.

Feelings of hopelessness may surface, as a recognizable sign of the entrapment resulting from repeated failure and frustration (e.g., "No matter what I do, he won't listen!"). Or, alternatively, parents may express rigid adherence to their belief that everything will rapidly disintegrate if they loosen the grip that keeps them in tenuous control of the stress in their lives (e.g., "He only listens to me if I really get mad and threaten to let him have it!"). The parent-child relationship has had ample opportunity to become shaped through aversive control procedures, and both members find it difficult to escape from this style of interaction.

There is certainly some element of truth in the parent's perception that they are "trapped" into continuing to use harsh forms of control with the child. Some children easily habituate to existing levels of punishment intensity, so that more and more harsh forms of discipline are required to attain the previous level of compliance or desired behavior. Moreover, the short-term consequences for the parent may serve to maintain strict control over the child. For example, such control may ease the parent's tension and frustration (i.e., negative reinforcement), and provide the parent with immediate obedience from the child or similar forms of positive reinforcement. These immediate "gains" may outweigh the less noticeable, long-term consequences of this negative cycle: the need to increase the intensity of the punishment to maintain strict control, the child's avoidance of the parent and susceptability to emotional and physical harm, and the failure of this process to teach the child the desired behaviors that would eliminate much of the need to rely on punishment methods.

Compensatory Factors Affecting
Outcome at Different Stages

The accumulation of negative events and poor coping responses that lead over time to the increased probability of child abuse are dependent to some extent upon the absence or failure of important compensatory factors. Clearly, many parents who face socioeconomic pressures and poor preparation for the parenting role are not entirely consumed by these processes. Although the potential number of compensatory factors is limitless, several highly significant ones can be identified on the basis of the parenting and child abuse literatures previously discussed (see Belsky, 1984; Maccoby & Martin, 1983).

During the early formation of the parent-child relationship and the initial establishment of a parenting style (Stage I), financial and marital stability within the family unit certainly portends a more successful and favorable outcome. A supportive spouse may be capable of offsetting some of the confusion and irritation that the other parent may express in attempting to meet his or her role demands and own expectations. Adequate social supports, positive parenting models, and suitable resources also frequently accompany families who have stabilized their financial situation and have settled into the community. Along these same lines, parents who experience success and mastery in their educational and career goals are accomplishing tasks that have a bearing on their self-esteem, self-efficacy and ultimately on their sense of parenting competence. During Stage I, therefore, these major factors are believed to play a significant role in counterbalancing the stressful nature of family and child-rearing responsibilities.

Stage II represents a period in which stressful circumstances are having a significant impact on the parent's interactive style with the child. The degree of stress experienced by the parent, however, can be readily offset by factors in the family, the community, or those related to the parent's approach to coping. Improvement in the child's behavior represents one of the most highly salient compensatory factors during this period. For example, the child's behavior may change for the better (through maturation, treatment, change in family circumstances, or similar events), leading the parent to reduce his or her use of strict control and to associate the child with pleasant events and attractive characteristics. The community may offer resources to the family that accelerate improvement in parent-child relations, such as subsidized day-care facilities, educational and treatment programs for parents and children, employment training opportunities, and so forth. Finally, not the least significant is the parents' evaluation of their coping resources, options, and the potential for control of stressful events. Folkman (1984) explains that coping resources may be psychological (e.g., problem-solving skills, an optimistic outlook, high self-esteem), social (e.g., social support systems for emotional and informational needs), physical (e.g., stamina, energy, health), or material (e.g., money, transportation). Therefore, even if a situation is initially perceived as stressful, the overall impact of the event can be reduced if the appropriate coping resources are made available.

Unfortunately, compensatory factors are minimal once a parent has progressed to the abusive style denoted by Stage III. However, despite the propensity to justify the use of physical control techniques under a wide range of circumstances, such practices may be retrenched by individual or community efforts. The parent, for example, may become dissatisfied with the outcome of physical punishment (either through the influence of someone else or through his/her own recognition), and feel an urgent need to refrain from using this method. Conversely, the child may begin to respond more favorably to parental directives, and the coercive cycle may start to dissipate. Community efforts to curtail child abuse may also have an impact on the perpetuation of high-risk practices in some instances. This is especially evident when the parents are "caught" and warned of their intolerable behavior as soon as the crisis point has been reached, and services are immediately put into place to supplement the parent's coping resources and reduce the level of stress. These compensatory factors augment one another, so that the presence of several supportive resources stands the maximum chance of eliminating child abuse in any given situation.

4

PSYCHOLOGICAL CHARACTERISTICS OF ABUSIVE PARENTS

Ever since child abuse was identified as a serious problem in the early 1960s, a great deal of interest has been directed toward discovering the psychological makeup of parents who harm their own children. Because the vast majority of parents are capable of dealing with the demands of their role without resorting to power assertion or violence, concerns that abusive parents lack some form of inner control, show little concern about their role as parents, or have distorted beliefs about the importance of harsh discipline have been paramount. Paradoxically, all of these suspicions have in one way or another been supported by research studies. Yet a *distinctive* psychological profile of abusive parents seems less and less likely to emerge (Green, 1978; Spinetta & Rigler, 1972).

The reasons for this lack of consensus regarding parental characteristics center primarily on the knowledge that child abuse is an *interactional event* that depends to some extent upon situational factors that elicit parental reactions. Personality characteristics of abusive parents are more broad ranging (from minor to major psychopathology) than initially suspected, and such characteristics interact with innumerable factors to produce the behavior of concern. In order to establish a psychological profile of abusive parents, therefore, it is necessary to understand such behavior within the context in which it occurs, the background from which it was derived, and the existing child-rearing norms that tolerate certain levels of violence between family members.

In addition, this interactional viewpoint implies that abusive parents are not a homogeneous group that shares a number of psychological characteristics that differ from other parents. To the contrary, few studies have found abusive parents to differ significantly on major psychological dimensions when compared with nonabusive parents from similar sociodemographic backgrounds (Wolfe, 1985a). The attitudinal, behavioral, emotional, and cognitive differences that have been linked to child abusers appear to be less conspicuous and pathological than previously assumed on the basis of descriptions of their actions. On the other hand, the distinctions (in personality functioning, parenting style, family interactions, and so on) that have been detected between abusive and nonabusive parents help to explain some of the processes underlying this complex and deviant behavior.

OVERVIEW OF CLINICAL AND
EMPIRICAL DESCRIPTIONS OF ABUSIVE PARENTS

Early case reports and uncontrolled clinical investigations of abusive parents focused primarily upon the underlying personality dimensions believed to be responsible for this phenomenon. Clinical descriptions that were documented in these early studies provided a valuable foundation for continued investigation, although some of the earlier conclusions have been challenged by subsequent findings. As shown in Table 4.1, these early studies provided initial descriptions of behavioral and cognitive-emotional dimensions of personality that established several important precedents in the research and clinical literature. Most notably, researchers surmised that abusers' interpersonal behavior was marked by social isolation, impulsivity, chronic aggressivity, and limited parenting skills. Abusers' cognitive and emotional adjustment was believed to differ from other parents in terms of a low frustration tolerance, emotional immaturity, inappropriate expressions of anger, role reversal with the child (that is, looking to the child to fulfill one's own needs), feelings of inadequacy and low self-esteem, and unrealistic expectations for child behavior.

As more investigators from various disciplines began to enter the field of child abuse research in the 1970s, some of the earlier views of abusive parents began to give way to new empirical findings. In particular, the concept of a "personality disorder" proved to be of little value in differentiating abusive and nonabusive parents, mostly due to the broad range of personality dimensions or descriptions that often emerged from studies of this population. In place of personality

TABLE 4.1
Psychological Characteristics of Abusive Parents
Reported in Early Clinical Studies

I. *Behavioral Dimension*
- Chronically aggressive (9)
- Isolated from family and friends (11)
- Rigid and domineering (9, 11)
- Impulsive (3, 4, 7, 11, 12)
- Experiencing marital difficulties (7)

II. *Cognitive-Emotional Dimension*
- Emotional immaturity (11)
- Low frustration tolerance (4, 7, 11, 12)
- Difficulty expressing anger (4, 7, 11, 12)
- Role reversal; looks to child to gratify own needs (2, 4, 5, 6, 10)
- Child misbehavior triggers feelings of inadequacy, worthlessness, frustration (11)
- Deficits in self-esteem (1, 2, 5)
- Inability to empathize with children (6, 8)
- High expectations of child; disregard for child's needs and abilities (6, 8, 10)
- Defends "right" to use physical punishment (12)
- Deep resentment toward own parents for failing to satisfy dependency needs (8)

NOTE: The following references to original studies are representative and not exhaustive. Most findings involved inferences drawn from clinical samples, without control group comparisons: (1) Bell (1973); (2) Blumberg (1974); (3) Elmer (1963); (4) Green (1976); (5) Green et al. (1974); (6) Helfer (1973); (7) Kempe et al. (1962); (8) Melnick & Hurley (1969); (9) Merrill (1962); (10) Morris & Gould (1963); (11) Steele & Pollock (1968); (12) Wasserman (1967). Also, see reviews by Green (1978); Kelly (1983); Parke & Collmer (1975); and Spinetta & Rigler (1972).

dimensions, empirical studies focused more directly on rates of behavior between family members, as well as comparative self-reports relating to perceptions of their children, physical and emotional symptomatology that may interfere with parental abilities, and emotional reactivity to stressful child-rearing situations.

Table 4.2 summarizes the findings of empirical studies that have involved matched control groups (families who are comparable on sociodemographic variables) and psychometric approaches to assessing abusive parents. What first emerges from a careful comparison of the earlier clinical reports and these subsequent empirical studies is an overlap of findings in several key areas, which strengthens some of the clinically derived assumptions about the psychological characteristics of abusive parents. In particular, recent studies have reaffirmed earlier reports of behavioral differences in terms of (a) low frustration tolerance

TABLE 4.2
Psychological Characteristics of Abusive Parents
Reported in Recent Empirical Studies

I. *Behavioral Dimension*
   - Isolation from family and friends (19, 20)
   - Less communication and less child stimulation (7, 8)
   - Disproportionate rate of negative to positive interactions with other family members (3, 4, 11, 13, 16, 17)
   - Failure to match disciplinary methods to child's transgression; intrusive, inconsistent (16, 23)

II. *Cognitive-Emotional Dimension*
   - Self-described as unhappy, rigid, distressed (11, 15)
   - More self-expressed anger (15, 20)
   - Child's behavior perceived as stressful (9, 14, 22, 25)
   - Low frustration tolerance, that is, greater emotional (psychophysiological) reactivity to child provocation (7, 9, 24)
   - Inappropriate expectations of child: disregard for child's needs and abilities; for example, belief that child intentionally annoys parent (1, 2, 12, 20; exceptions: 18, 21)
   - Greater *perceived* life stress (5, 14, 18)
   - Flattened affect during parent-child interactions (16)

III. *Other Findings Related to Psychological Functioning*
   - More physical health problems (5, 11)

IV. *Empirical Findings that Did Not Differ from Controls*
   - *Amount* of stressful life events (10, 21)
   - Self-expressed emotional needs; for example, feeling unloved; dependency; emotional problems, or personal adjustment (5, 10, 21, 26; exception: 11)
   - Denial of problems (10)

NOTE: The following studies used matched control groups to compare responses of abusive parents to nonabusive parents from similar backgrounds (see review by Wolfe, 1985a): (1) Azar et al. (1984); (2) Bauer & Twentyman (1985); (3) Bousha & Twentyman (1984); (4) Burgess & Conger (1978); (5) Conger et al. (1979); (6) Crittenden & Bonvillian (1984); (7) Disbrow et al. (1977); (8) Dietrich et al. (1980); (9) Frodi & Lamb (1980); (10) Gaines et al. (1978); (11) Lahey et al. (1984); (12) Larrance & Twentyman (1983); (13) Lorber et al. (1984); (14) Mash et al. (1983); (15) Milner & Wimberley (1980); (16) Oldershaw et al. (1986); (17) Reid et al. (1981); (18) Rosenberg & Reppucci (1983); (19) Salzinger et al. (1983); (20) Spinetta (1978); (21) Starr (1982); (22) Susman et al. (1985); (23) Trickett & Kuczynski (1986); (24) Wolfe et al. (1983); (25) Wolfe & Mosk (1983); (26) Wright (1976).

and inappropriate expressions of anger (as measured by emotional reactivity to provocative child stimuli), (b) social isolation from important sources of support, and (c) impaired parenting skills (e.g., inconsistent, unstimulating, inflexible). Furthermore, on the cognitive-behavioral dimension, abusers have been found by recent investigators (d) to demonstrate unrealistic expectations of their children, (e) to report that their child's behavior is very stressful to them, and (f) to describe themselves as being inadequate or incompetent in their role as parents.

However, several of the earlier descriptions of abusive parents have not been confirmed or have not been suitably investigated. This outcome is not surprising in that many of the previous personality constructs were difficult to define and measure, such as impulsivity, emotional immaturity, and self-esteem. Regrettably, abusive *fathers* have seldom been involved in research studies, which has limited any conclusions regarding male-female differential characteristics or the significance of marital problems in the etiology of abuse. Furthermore, with the addition of matched nonabusive control groups, many researchers were finding that these nonabusive but disadvantaged families also reported many of the same child behavior problems, negative childhood experiences, and general dissatisfaction as did parents who were reported for child abuse. Thus, as stated previously, many of the psychological characteristics of abusive parents have to be viewed as only predispositions (or "abuse-proneness"; Green, 1978), with the corollary that a child and a stress-filled environment are necessary situational determinants of abuse.

Rather than discovering a distinctive personality profile or cluster of symptomatology, what has emerged from comparative investigations of abusive and nonabusive parents is a better understanding of behavior patterns of abusive parents that are inflexible and maladaptive in certain situational contexts, such as dealing with difficult child behavior, problem solving with other family members, and handling chronic levels of stress. These studies of behavioral, cognitive, and emotional characteristics of abusive parents, along with their underlying rationales, provide the focus of the remainder of this chapter.

INTERPERSONAL BEHAVIOR IN
FAMILY AND SOCIAL SETTINGS

It is disturbing to note that rates of violence between family members are higher than for any other social group (Gelles & Straus, 1979). Researchers studying child-abusive and spouse-abusive families have frequently reported hitting, overt conflict, and disharmony in the family setting (Straus et al., 1980) that seems to continue unchecked unless serious injury is reported, or one family member decides to "break tradition" and disrupt the cycle through departure, legal charges, or therapeutic intervention. This situation is somewhat understandable (but still intolerable) if consideration is given to the nature of the family. The family setting is one in which ascribed roles, lack of privacy, high levels of stress, and the implicit acceptance of violence may converge upon the individual's coping ability at any point in time and result in inappropriate or desperate efforts to restore equilibrium.

Awareness of the extent of conflict and violence between family members (both adults and children) has increased dramatically in recent years, along with the recognition that child abuse often coexists with other forms of family violence. For example, interviews conducted with a nationwide sample of 1146 persons living with a partner and children revealed that previous exposure to harsh physical punishment as a child and marital disharmony and violence as an adult were significantly associated with higher rates of severe violence toward children (Straus, 1980a, 1980b). Straus and his colleagues (Straus et al., 1980) were struck by the realization that child abuse, as well as other forms of family violence, are not due to some extremely abnormal or pathological influence. To the contrary, they concluded:

> While granting that some instances of intrafamily violence are an outgrowth of social or psychological pathology, we maintain that physical violence between family members is a normal part of family life in most societies, and in American society in particular. (Gelles & Straus, 1979, p. 549)

It appears, moreover, that violence in one sphere of life tends to carry over into other spheres, a conclusion that is supported by two major sources of research information: (1) the recognition of patterns of abuse across generations, and (2) observations of behavioral interactions between members of physically abusive families.

Patterns of Intergenerational Abuse

Being a victim of child abuse or the indirect victim of interparental violence (through the witnessing of severe conflict and violence between parents) has long been associated with the perpetuation of a cycle of violence across generations. Abusive parents often report retrospectively that they were mistreated or abused during their own childhood (Kempe & Helfer, 1972; Spinetta & Rigler, 1972), and violent delinquents similarly report that they were raised in an atmosphere of violence and low affectional expression (e.g., Lewis, Pincus, & Glaser, 1979; Tarter, Hegedus, Winsten, & Alterman, 1984). These clinical case studies and retrospective investigations led the Canadian government to conclude in their report on aggressive and delinquent behavior that violence in one's family background is the most commonly cited predictor of future violent behavior on the part of the individual (Standing Senate Committee on Health, Welfare, & Science, 1980).

Despite the strong influence that violence in one's past may have on future behavior, only a small minority (less than 15%) of adults who report being abused as children were themselves found to be abusive toward their own children. This finding was reported in the nationwide interview study conducted by Straus et al. (1980), in which parents were asked to describe the parenting methods that they recalled from their childhood, as well as their own current parental methods used to discipline or resolve conflicts. Apparently, a number of positive influences, such as supportive adults, siblings, successful achievements at school, and so on may serve over time to moderate the effect of abuse or related childhood stressors. Moreover, as discussed in Chapter 5, the long-term effects of physical abuse or neglect must be considered in relation to concomitant psychological injuries to the child that also can be very damaging, such as rejection, lack of affection, and exposure to dangerous situations. Therefore, we may cautiously conclude that previous childhood experiences involving abuse and family violence *predispose* an individual to using similar methods during adulthood, with an associated increase of approximately three to five times over the base rate of child abuse in the population.

Within this intergenerational context, parenting can be viewed as an adaptational challenge that is influenced by prior experiences and resources (Sroufe & Rutter, 1984). This developmental viewpoint of parenting suggests that earlier forms of behavior (such as the use of threats and physical aggression with peers) become hierarchically integrated with more complex, recent forms of behavior and remain potentially active, especially in periods of stress. For example, a parent who failed to develop self-control during childhood and adolescence may fall back on using aggressive behavior when threatened or frustrated by current events. Moreover, it is assumed by developmental researchers that the more recently integrated patterns of behavior are the most susceptible to disruption, giving way to the earlier, less differentiated forms that are often more problematic.

The implication of this developmental viewpoint is that a disordered pattern of adaptation may lie dormant until periods of extreme stress (such as child-rearing demands or family circumstances) elicit the expression of previous patterns. Furthermore, this viewpoint implies that previous modes of functioning are currently available to assist or hinder a person's adaptation to new situations. Thus persons who are inflexible in their use of previously acquired maladaptive behavior patterns are most likely to fail the challenge of new adaptational tasks, such as child rearing and family functioning. A large number of abusive parents certainly fall within the realm of such a descriptive account.

Interactions Between Family Members

Physical violence between intimates such as family members is an event that is seldom witnessed by dispassionate observers or social scientists. From reconstructed events and interviews investigators have established a descriptive understanding of what occurs under these circumstances, but a more in-depth analysis of the processes related to interpersonal aggression and violence requires an ongoing documentation of sequential interactions between participants. Thus researchers have chosen to observe members of physically abusive families under a wide range of common or typical family circumstances that may provide a close approximation of the manner in which adults and children behave. This approach to studying the behavior of abusive parents has advanced our knowledge of *what* behavior is being shown most often (and under what circumstances), leading to a clearer picture of the relationship between everyday interactions and severe conflict and abuse. Typically, investigators interested in family interactions have narrowed their focus to allow for more detailed analyses of specific concerns, such as a parent's reactions to a child's demands at home. At times, observation periods are structured to increase the likelihood of observing parent-child interactions of greatest interest (such as a teaching or compliance task), while some researchers choose to observe families with only a minimum amount of interference or structure.

Results of these observational studies have indicated that one of the most significant behavioral characteristics of abusive parents is their *disproportionate expression of negative or aversive behavior toward members of their own family.* Whereas physical abuse per se is a relatively infrequent event, members of abusive families more commonly engage in other forms of less extreme conflict and mutual antagonism (e.g., criticisms, threats, shouting) that is suggestive of family dysfunction. Observations revealed that members of abusive families were not necessarily more aversive toward one another on an absolute basis, but were *proportionately more negative than positive* in the tone of their interactions. That is, the overall rate of interaction between all members of abusive families was significantly lower than nonabusive controls, so that when members did choose to interact there was an imbalance in their rate of positive and negative behavioral expression.

For example, in the presence of observers, members of abusive families spoke to one another less often, engaged in activities with one another infrequently, and generally tended to avoid or ignore one another. When interactions did occur between family members, they were likely to involve efforts to maintain control or place demands on other adult or child members (see Burgess & Conger, 1978; Lahey et al., 1984; Lorber, Felton, & Reid, 1984; Oldershaw et al., 1986; Reid, Taplin, & Lorber, 1981). However, comparisons of abusive families with other distressed (but nonabusive) groups of parents have revealed that abusive families are not necessarily unique in their patterns of family conflict in that some distressed families also exhibit higher rates of aversive exchanges and proportionately more negative than positive behavior (Lorber et al., 1984).

These observational studies helped to clarify long-held suspicions that members of abusive families are more conflictual and coercive toward one another, although this conclusion was reached in a manner that differed from initial theoretical contentions. That is, it appears to be the relative absence of positive interactions that sets members of abusive families apart from matched, nonabusive controls rather than the dramatic display of open conflict and aggression (Wolfe, 1985a). Family members may learn to minimize their interactions in an effort to avoid conflict, since minor conflicts can quickly develop into large-scale attack. Unfortunately, the avoidance of interaction carries with it the absence of prosocial, desirable exchanges that could serve to reverse or attenuate expectations of conflict. The everyday style of interaction observed between members of abusive families therefore suggests that impairments in methods of adult-adult and parent-child communication and problem solving may be causal or contributing factors to abuse.

Child-Rearing Patterns and Parenting Skills

The vast majority of incidents investigated by child protective service agencies involve inappropriate actions by the parent to gain control of the child, which rapidly become dangerous and harmful (Herrenkohl et al., 1983; Kadushin & Martin, 1981). Thus the most widely investigated issue related to interactions in abusive families is the suspicion that such parents are significantly more punitive and harsh toward their children on a day-to-day basis or are less appropriate in their choices of disciplinary methods.

Concerns about the punitive or insensitive nature of the parent-child relationship have been addressed separately by theorists interested in both the social-interactional and the psychopathological viewpoints. From a social-interactional perspective, findings regarding aversive and inappropriate parent-child interactions support the contention that abusers use ineffective punishment contingencies and fail to respond to prosocial behavior. Likewise, such findings are compatible with the position that abusers suffer from a pronounced impulse disorder or characterological defect that is expressed across a wide range of child-rearing situations.

Effective parenting, as discussed in Chapter 2, is characterized by flexibility such that the parent responds to the needs of the child and the situation. In practice, an effective parent is considered to be one who is relatively successful in gaining compliance from a child, and whose child exhibits age-appropriate levels of competence in areas of social development. Effective parents enforce house rules in a consistent and firm manner by using commands and sanctions when necessary, expect and set age-appropriate standards for mature behavior, use reasoning when giving directives and discipline, and encourage independence and individual expression (Maccoby & Martin, 1983). In contrast, studies reveal that abusive parents rely on ineffective child-management techniques as measured by their lower rates of consistent, prosocial behavior during common child-rearing tasks. Similar to the previously reported findings on interactions between all members of abusive families, observational studies reveal that abusive parents are not necessarily *more aversive* or punitive toward their children on a daily basis, but when they choose to interact with their children they are more likely (than nonabusive controls) to do so in an aversive, negative fashion as opposed to using more positive methods.

Several areas of child rearing have been assessed through clinic and home observations of abusive parents and their children in an attempt to identify the patterns of interaction that might differentiate abusive from nonabusive parents (see Table 4.2). In general, these studies endorse the view that abusive parents are ineffectual in their attempts to teach new behavior or to control undesirable behavior with their children, and fail to exhibit sensitive and stimulating care to their offspring. Moreover, such findings emerge in observational studies of abusive parents across the full range of child development.

Regarding interactions between abusive parents and their young infants, studies reveal that abusers use fewer modes of stimulation (such as pointing when directing or orienting the infant to the task; Dietrich, Starr, & Kaplan, 1980) and are extremely insensitive to their infants' cues and signals (Crittenden & Bonvillian, 1984). In the latter study, for example, 59 mother-infant dyads defined separately as abusive, neglectful, mentally retarded, deaf, low income, and middle income were compared on a number of indicants of maternal sensitivity (e.g., responsive facial expression, rhythmic voice tone, clear, consistent commands). The researchers noted that an abusive mother would "suddenly move her face or toy in close to her baby's face, producing a startle or wince. The mother also would often tease her baby by jabbing or poking at the infant, and would frequently interfere with her baby's play" (1984, p. 259). It is interesting to note as well that neglecting mothers were found to be generally uninvolved and passive, whereas abusing mothers were more active, interfering, and occasionally openly hostile.

Studies focusing on parenting skills involving toddler and preschool-aged children find similarly ineffective or insensitive methods being employed by abusive parents during common, everyday child-rearing situations. Specifically, abusive parents show fewer facilitative and communication skills (such as specific commands and explanations for the child; Disbrow, Doerr, & Caulfield, 1977), fewer physical and positive behaviors (such as handing an object to the child or praising the child; Bousha & Twentyman, 1984; Burgess & Conger, 1978), and less positive affect during interactions with their children (such as smiling or hugging; Lahey et al., 1984; Oldershaw et al., 1986).

Further evidence of the ineffectiveness of parenting methods among abusive samples emerges from studies investigating parents' choices of disciplinary techniques and their relative success in obtaining child compliance. Reid et al. (1981), in a comparison of attempts to achieve child compliance among samples of abusive, nondistressed, and nonabusive parents who were experiencing child behavior problems, found that the nondistressed parents were successful in 86% of their command attempts, the nonabusive, behavior problem parents were successful in 65% of their attempts, while the abusive parents were successful only 46% of the time. Trickett & Kuczynski (1986) approached this same issue by having parents keep a diary of conflict situations that arose at home over a five-day period. Abusive parents reported using punitive approaches, such as yelling and threatening, regardless of the type of child misbehavior, whereas nonabusive parents' choices of disciplinary techniques were more aligned with the type of misbehavior, such as ignoring fussing behavior and diverting the child's attention to appropriate activity. It is of interest that these latter researchers noted that abused children were less likely to comply with their parents' initial request for compliance than nonabused children, and that when abused children failed to comply they often were more verbally disruptive and demanding.

On the basis of these observational studies, it appears that abusive parents fail to use effective parenting techniques that would reduce problematic child behaviors and increase desirable behaviors. However, this conclusion is distinct from the implied assumption that abusers are more aversive or harsh toward their children during everyday interactions. Investigations of abusers' rates of aversive behavior toward their children (e.g., threats, humiliation, grabbing) have produced equivocal findings, with two studies showing no differences in rates (Burgess & Conger, 1978; Mash, Johnston, & Kovitz, 1983), two studies showing differences between abusive and nondistressed parents, but not between abusive and distressed parents (Reid et al., 1981; Lorber et al., 1984), and three studies finding significantly higher rates of aggressive and power-assertive behavior among abusers than among controls (Bousha & Twentyman, 1984; Lahey et al., 1984; Oldershaw et al., 1986). To explain this inconsistency, it is important to consider the nature of parent-child interactions in disadvantaged families. Both abusive and nonabusive parents may criticize, scold, threaten, or punish their children following common transgressions; however, abusive parents often have been found to respond negatively as well to the child's *prosocial behavior* (Wolfe, 1985a). Furthermore, abusers tend to *reciprocate* the child's aversive behavior rather than attempt to decrease or punish such behavior in an effective manner, thus serving to maintain the coercive exchanges so often found among this population.

Social Incompetence and Isolation from Support Systems

Investigators have suggested that the behavior shown by abusive parents toward other family members may be indicative of a more pervasive, problematic style of interaction. This concern originated from early clinical descriptions of abusive parents that emphasized their isolation from individuals and community resources (Steele & Pollock, 1968), and their general discomfort expressed in interpersonal situations

(Kempe & Helfer, 1972). Continued reports of such extreme social isolation have rekindled interests aimed at discovering the individual and social phenomena responsible for child maltreatment beyond the family context.

Several studies have assessed abusive parents' perceptions of whether other people are available and willing to listen to their problems and/or provide moral support and assistance. Their findings generally concur with early clinical impressions that abusers tend to avoid social contacts and fail to develop positive support networks. For example, Garbarino and Crouter (1978) found that parents who were isolated from important social support systems in their neighborhoods, such as churches, recreational centers, or family-oriented activities, were more likely to become abusive to their children than those who had ready access to such supports. Similarly, abusers were found to be more isolated from supports, especially peer networks, and to spend less time with the persons that they identify as being a part of their peer support network (Salzinger et al., 1983). Thus the significance of social isolation and the limited availability of social supports in relation to abusive families is relatively straightforward—inappropriate child-rearing values and methods, such as the use of harsh physical discipline, may be perpetuated in the absence of more appropriate models and assistance (Parke & Collmer, 1975; Spinetta & Rigler, 1972).

Knowledge of the importance of social supports in the parenting role has raised a number of questions concerning what factors produce or maintain such isolation. Burgess (1985) argues that the maladaptive interactional style often shown by abusive parents toward their children is representative of their general interpersonal skills. This emphasis on interactional style shares some resemblance to the notion of a global psychiatric disorder or personality trait that pervades the parents' daily interactions in that it could involve a characterological "defect" or disturbance that is causally linked to abusive behavior. However, an important distinction between psychiatric disturbance and lack of interpersonal skills is raised by involving the concept of *social competence*. Social competence can be defined as the ability to interact effectively with the environment through the use of interpersonal skills that elicit a positive response from the other person (Burgess, 1985; Wolfe, 1985b). To be socially competent, a person must show some capacity to behave in a positive fashion toward others, such as praising, complimenting, or showing affection. Additionally, a person must be able to observe the demands of a situation in order to choose the appropriate action, and he or she must be able to behave in a fashion that is rewarding to both interactants (Burgess & Youngblade, in press).

Based on clinical descriptions and correlational studies, abusive parents often behave poorly on several of the above dimensions of social competence that involve interactions with others both within and outside of the family. That is, abusers are more likely to be poor observers of child behavior, to respond in a noncontingent fashion to the demands of child rearing, to exhibit disproportionately more negative than positive behavior toward other family members, and to show a pattern of social isolation, poor work history, and fewer friendships with others outside of the home. As a consequence, researchers have speculated that general deficiencies in social skills, combined with unmanageable stress, may be responsible for the lack of social supports found among abusive families (Burgess, 1985; Salzinger et al., 1983). This lack of social support and involvement with others in the community in turn maintains the individual's propensity to resolve interpersonal situations by relying on his or her own "independence" (that is, refusing to consider alternative strategies or assistance), by avoiding situations that may be stressful, or by using coercive tactics to resolve conflicts.

It has also been argued that abusive parents isolate themselves from unnecessary contacts with others in the community as a way of coping with the large number of difficult, stressful events encountered in their daily environments. Under circumstances of limited economic resources, overcrowding, unemployment, and so on some parents may prefer to isolate themselves as much as possible from unnecessary contacts with others. This relationship between social stress and social isolation has been termed "insularity" (Dumas & Wahler, 1985; Wahler, 1980), characterized by a high level of negatively perceived interchanges and a low level of positively perceived interchanges with others in the community. During everyday activities, for example, abusive parents were found to interact more often with people in similar situations to themselves (such as friends and relatives with parenting difficulties and stressful circumstances) rather than forming a support network that could provide assistance and emotional support (Wahler & Hann, 1984). Consequently, such parents become more despondent, irritable, and ineffective in their interactions with their children, and their propensity to use power-assertive, authoritarian parenting methods increases proportionately.

Furthermore, because abusive parents often fail to develop positive relationships (due to social incompetence, limited skills, high levels of stress, or other factors), they are more likely to perpetuate their negative exchanges with others and to extend their isolation from community resources. The concept of social competence therefore is useful for highlighting the importance of the interaction between situational and individual variables in determining the likelihood of child abuse. Situational variables such as aversive contacts with others in the family or community, combined with individual characteristics such as limited social competence and interpersonal skills, may produce responses of anger and irritation that pose a significant risk to the child who must depend on his or her parent for attention, affection, and physical needs each day.

We may conclude from the preceding sections relating to child abusers' interpersonal behavior in family and social settings that although abusive parents may not manifest any distinguishable personality or psychiatric disorders, they do exhibit behavioral differences and a lack of social competence indicative of maladjustment in the parental role. In comparison to nonabusive parents, abusers are not as effective or successful in the parenting role, both in terms of teaching their children new behaviors as well as in controlling any behavior problems the child has. Abusive parents are less flexible in their choices of disciplinary techniques and often fail to match their choice of discipline to the child's misdeed and the situation. Their overreliance on physical punishment as a control strategy, in combination with limited child management skills, is intensified by their failure to develop social supports to alleviate stress and to assist in family problem solving.

COGNITIVE AND EMOTIONAL
CHARACTERISTICS OF ABUSIVE PARENTS

In general, observational studies presented previously have focused primarily upon a description of how abusive parents *react* to events or aversive stimuli. That is, parents may harm their children due to their ineffectiveness in managing child behavior or in response to anger and frustration related to their lack of social supports and assistance. However, attention to other psychological processes that may serve to mediate the expression of abusive behavior is also a high priority in developing an understanding of child abuse. Although child abusers rarely show severe psychiatric disorders—impairments such as major thought disorders, affect disturbance, or sociopathy are estimated to exist in approximately 5%-10% of the child abusive population

(Spinetta & Rigler, 1972; Starr, 1979; Steele & Pollock, 1968)—researchers and clinicians have long suspected that impaired emotional and cognitive processes play a major role in the expression of such deviant behavior.

This view is supported by a research consensus derived from other clinically distressed populations, indicating that psychological processes such as perceptions of others, evaluations and interpretations of events, and affective reactions to aversive situations serve to determine the behavioral response of the person (Lefcourt, 1973). Accordingly, these processes are presumed to play a major role in increasing or decreasing the likelihood of aggressive action toward a child. The importance of cognitive and emotional factors, therefore, will be explored in relation to the following three sections: (1) symptoms of emotional distress, (2) knowledge and expectations of children, and (3) emotional arousal and reactivity to child provocation.

Symptoms of Emotional Distress

The importance of the parent's psychological functioning in the etiology or maintenance of child abuse emerges from studies that have documented elevated reports of affective and somatic distress among abusive samples. Abusers have been found by several researchers to report elevated physical and emotional symptoms, such as dissatisfaction, irritation, physical health problems, and stressful child-rearing encounters (Conger, Burgess, and Barrett, 1979; Lahey et al., 1984; Mash et al., 1983). Although this symptomatology has seldom been of such severity and magnitude to meet the criteria of a psychiatric diagnosis or disorder, these symptoms of emotional distress most likely impair their functioning as parents.

Clinical accounts have also led to recent concerns that some abusive parents may suffer from high levels of depression, which may be partially responsible for the disturbance in the parent-child relationship. Symptoms of depression, such as sadness, irritability, withdrawal from social activities, guilt, lowered self-esteem, and similar signs of distress, are often used to describe the abusive parent (see Tables 4.1 and 4.2), and therefore may be especially likely to interfere with the development of the parent-child relationship. Rather than exhibiting the more common symptoms of depression (e.g., sadness, anhedonia, self-blame), however, it is suspected that the manner in which abusive parents manifest their symptoms of depression may be disguised by hostility, anger, and conflict with the child (Susman, Trickett, Iannotti, Hollenbeck, & Zahn-Waxler, 1985).

Limited support for this depression-abuse relationship was found in a comparative study of depressed (current and past; major and minor depression), abusive, and normal mothers (total N = 94) on self-reported child-rearing practices and values (Susman et al., 1985). High guilt induction and high anxiety induction (e.g., belief that punishment will find children if they are bad; belief that children should be aware of parental sacrifices) characterized both the abusive mothers (N = 18) and the mothers with current major depression (N = 10), although only the abusive mothers reported that these methods were used in conjunction with harsh, authoritarian practices. Whereas both the depressed and abusive mothers expressed more inconsistency, hostility, and protectiveness than the normal controls, it is noteworthy that the depressed mothers were much less deviant from the norm than were the abusive mothers on reported child-rearing attitudes and patterns.

We may cautiously conclude from these findings that a negative correlation exists between desirable socialization practices and maternal depression, yet abusive parents show even more pronounced deviance in socialization practices than depressed parents. Major depression and other forms of affect disturbance may play a role in establishing abusive practices by interfering with parental perceptions, attitudes, and values, yet the causal direction or significance of such a relationship has not been determined.

The findings above also direct our attention toward the importance of the *adult's perception of areas of stress* related to the parenting role. That is, one would expect to see some signs of emotional distress in persons who are exposed to a large number of aversive demands that they perceive as being uncontrollable and unpredictable (Johnson & Sarason, 1978). Evidence that this assumption applies to abusive parents has accumulated in the child abuse literature. Based on self-reported life events and symptomatology recent studies have found that, in the aggregate, abusive parents may not be subjected to significantly *more* socioeconomic disadvantage and life changes than matched control families (Gaines, Sandgrund, Green, & Power, 1978; Starr, 1982). However, the type and degree of life change associated with abusive families is more often *perceived* by these parents as extremely aversive and debilitating (Conger et al., 1979; Mash et al., 1983; Rosenberg & Reppucci, 1983).

The significance of parental perceptions or appraisal of stress in relation to behavioral and emotional expression is illustrated by two studies using quite different methodologies. Egeland et al. (1980), for example, assessed self-reported anxiety symptoms of maltreating (abuse and neglect) and nonmaltreating mothers using a prospective format, which allowed for a careful investigation of the relationship of life events and symptoms of distress to subsequent abuse or neglect. Whereas the *amount* of life stressors did not differentiate between the two groups, only the maltreating mothers reported experiencing significantly more anxiety in relation to these life changes.

Mash et al. (1983) studied the influence of specific child-rearing situations on abusive and nonabusive mothers by using an analog format that allowed for a manipulation of demands placed on the parents and children. When the two groups were asked to have their children complete a more demanding task (clean up toys, read numbers in sequence), abusive mothers were significantly more controlling and directive of their children than nonabusive mothers. When few demands were placed on the subjects, however, no significant differences between the groups emerged. These findings are in accord with several laboratory analog studies of child abuse that have manipulated maternal perceptions of environmental stressors and child responsiveness to parental directives. When mothers (who were nonabusive volunteers) perceived that the situation was becoming less controllable and more stressful, their rate of punitiveness toward the child increased dramatically (Mulhern & Passman, 1979; Vasta & Copitch, 1981).

In sum, empirical findings to date suggest that parental behaviors and symptoms of both overcontrol (e.g., depression, physical complaints) and undercontrol (e.g., aggression, verbal abuse) are possible reactions to, or precipitants of, child- and family-mediated stress. Individual characteristics, such as low tolerance for stress, inappropriate or inadequate models or learning opportunities, and a poor repertoire of life skills may be important psychological processes that are involved in determining the expression of these stressful life events. Furthermore, it is highly probable, on the basis of these findings, that abusive parents' perceptions of adverse family and environmental conditions are exacerbated by their failure to use social supports and to develop social networks, as discussed previously.

Perceptions and Expectations of Children

Early on, child abuse investigators recognized that parents' lack of awareness of children's needs and abilities may engender unusually high demands or distorted perceptions of their children's behavior (Kempe et al., 1962; Steele & Pollock, 1968). Practitioners observed that many abusive incidents involved senseless attempts by the parent to force a child to behave in a certain manner that was beyond the child's developmental limitations. This lack of awareness was believed to be due to immaturity, self-centeredness, role reversal, emotional deprivation during childhood, and similar intrinsic and acquired characteristics (see Table 4.1) that interfered with parental responsivity and expectations of their children. An abusive parent, according to initial theoretical reasonings, may perceive the child as a source of competition (for one's spouse, time, or similar desires), unrealistic dependency, or excessive stress, which justifies his or her inappropriate methods of discipline and expectations.

What psychological characteristics could be responsible for such extreme distortions in parental expectations? Bypassing the possibility of a major thought disorder such as schizophrenia (which seems to be seldom evident among abusive parents), at least three viable explanations can account for this important phenomenon. One of the earliest, single-factor explanations to be stated in this regard postulated that general deficits in parental knowledge and understanding of normal child development and child care were due to *low adult intelligence* (e.g., Fisher, 1958; Simpson, 1967). More recently, Crittenden and Bonvillian (1984) discovered in their review of factors associated with maternal risk of child maltreatment a range of 30% to 77% of borderline or subnormal intelligence reported in samples of abusing and neglecting parents. However, lower intelligence is more commonly associated with child neglect than abuse (Polansky, Chalmers, Buttenweiser, & Williams, 1981), and these two types of maltreatment have seldom been distinguished adequately. Thus, although limited intelligence may be implicated in some instances of physical abuse, the relative etiological importance of this factor has been strongly disputed (Spinetta & Rigler, 1972). Evidence as to its sole importance is lacking, which suggests that intelligence may be involved in the etiology of child abuse mainly in terms of its interaction with other parental characteristics and learning opportunities, such as the acquisition of parenting skills and child-rearing information.

A second explanation for the purported link between child abuse and parental perceptions and expectations of the child began to evolve in the 1960s. This approach relied less heavily on general intelligence as a causal factor and focused more specifically upon deficits related to child-rearing knowledge and attitudes. Abusive parents were believed to be incapable of empathizing with their children and to show a general disregard for a child's needs and abilities (Helfer, 1973; Melnick & Hurley, 1969; Morris & Gould, 1963). This disregard for children was linked to their own deprived childhood and/or lack of acquired interest in children. Despite the intuitive appeal of this explanation, however, several studies exploring this issue failed to differentiate abusers from nonabusers on attitudinal or perceptual dimensions. For example, results of self-report questionnaires tapping parents' knowledge of developmental milestones, discipline choices, or expectations of children (Gaines et al., 1978; Milner & Wimberley, 1980; Spinetta, 1978; Starr, 1982) produced equivocal findings. Overall, these studies revealed that abusers knew *what* they should expect or do with young children, but the results failed to reveal *why* they did not apply this knowledge to their own child. Thus the notion of abusers having a preexisting deficit in knowledge of child development or a global disinterest or disregard for children has not been strongly supported in the literature (see Kravitz & Driscoll, 1983; Wolfe, 1985a).

Further evidence related to parental perceptions of children among child abusers has led to a more complete understanding of this relationship. Earlier attempts to associate parental knowledge and perceptions of children with abusive practices relied primarily upon general developmental milestones and expectations, which may have failed to assess fully the complexity of interactions with a child. An alternative explanation involves a learning process whereby salient child characteristics, such as noncompliance, voice tone, and facial expressions, become associated with parental feelings of frustration, poor coping, and low self-efficacy. This approach assumes that an abuser's perceptual/cognitive style with a child may be a learned pattern that serves to perpetuate conflict and disharmony. In particular, this interpretation takes into account parents' negative past experiences with their *own children* under similar stressful circumstances that ended unfavorably, under the assumption that such experiences strengthen parental beliefs of the child's disturbing and provoking nature.

Recent studies have supported this third explanation by approaching the issue of child perception through improved methodology that has included samples of real or simulated child behavior. For example, two well-designed studies using samples of abusive and nonabusive parents found that abusers were most likely to view their child as acting *intentionally to annoy them,* even when minimal information was provided as the basis for their judgments (Bauer & Twentyman, 1985; Larrance & Twentyman, 1983). When presented with highly salient cues of their own child's misbehavior (e.g., photographs, video or audio recordings), abusers tend to expect the worst from their child, thus perpetuating their feelings of stress and loss of control. A study by Azar et al. (1984) further distinguished between developmental knowledge, on the one hand, and the application of that knowledge during realistic situations with the child, on the other hand. Maltreating parents differed from controls when asked to rate the *appropriateness* of expecting various child behaviors (e.g., "There is nothing wrong with punishing a 9-month-old for crying too much"), yet their knowledge of developmental milestones (e.g., age range when a child is capable of learning to count, climb stairs, and so on) did not significantly differ from other parents.

The clinical implications of these findings are important to consider. In relation to assessment, parents' idiosyncratic perceptions and expectations regarding their own child's behavior can best be identified during realistic child situations, rather than less salient recall or self-report. Presenting the parent with videotaped excerpts of child transgressions (based either on recorded interactions with their own child or a similar child), for example, may reveal the parent's unrealistic expectations or demands of the child (Wolfe, in press). In relation to treatment, it is important to consider that the parent may fail to acknowledge positive changes in child behavior or development due to the well-established learning history between the parent and child. Efforts to modify the parent's attitudes and behavior toward the child therefore should proceed in a manner that provides the parent with positive feedback for their initial attempts (e.g., simple play activities, observing child-therapist interactions) rather than attempting to challenge the parent's perspective or attitudes in an abstract fashion.

Emotional Arousal and Reactivity to Child Provocation

A major premise of the transitional model of child abuse presented in Chapter 3 involves the role of arousal in a stressful situation. Negative arousal, such as increased respiration, pulse rate, and muscular tension, may lead to aggression if the person labels the source of such arousal as anger provoking. Moreover, negative arousal interferes with rational problem solving, such that the person's awareness of the intensity of his or her actions becomes blurred by the urgency of retaliation.

Acts of interpersonal aggression appear to be highly attributable to situational cues and characteristics of the individual (see Averill, 1983; Berkowitz, 1983; Zillman, 1979). In the case of child abuse, in particular, the situational cues often involve aversive behavior or features of the child, and the presumed individual characteristics include such factors as oversensitivity (Knutson, 1978), disinhibition of aggression (Zillman, 1979), and limited interpersonal skills (Burgess, 1985). Early child abuse researchers advanced the importance of these emotionally related phenomena through their descriptions of abusive parents as impulsive and exhibiting a low frustration tolerance (Green, 1976; Kempe et al., 1962; Steele & Pollock, 1968).

These early reports, coupled with laboratory studies on aggressive behavior, sparked several investigators to measure abusive parents' emotional reactivity to difficult child behavior. Frodi & Lamb (1980), for example, showed videotaped scenes of smiling and crying infants to abusive subjects and matched controls, anticipating that abusers would show greater discomfort, irritation, and emotional arousal in the presence of such stimuli. In response to infant cries and smiles, abusive subjects evidenced greater physiological arousal (increased skin conductance, blood pressure, and heart rate) and reported more negative affect (more annoyance and indifference, and less sympathy) to both the crying and smiling infant scenes. Similarly, Wolfe, Fairbank, Kelly, and Bradlyn (1983) presented abusive and nonabusive parents with scenes of videotaped parent-child interactions, some of which were highly stressful (e.g., a child screaming and refusing to comply with her parent) and some of which were nonstressful (e.g., watching television quietly). As anticipated, abusive subjects responded to the stressful scenes with greater negative psychophysiological arousal than did the nonabusive comparison group (no group differences were found during the nonstressful scenes).

Although firm conclusions cannot be reached on the basis of these two preliminary studies, they provide initial evidence for the contention that emotional arousal and reactivity play a crucial role in the manifestation of abusive parenting. This pattern of arousal is presumed to develop over time as a function of problems in the parent-child relationship, whereby a parent may become respondently conditioned to experience negative arousal and emotions when interacting with his or her child (even when the child is behaving in a quiet or pleasant manner). This conditioning, or learning, process may occur over an undetermined time period; that is, either gradually, such as during early parent-infant contact or struggles, or suddenly, such as during high-stress periods in which the parent is less tolerant of child behavior or experiences an extremely difficult encounter with the child. However, such an arousal pattern has not been linked to any particular personality variables or situational events per se—it appears to be an idiosyncratic pattern that emerges as a function of an individual's predisposition (e.g., exposure to violence as a child, emotional distress) and his or her learning experience. Although researchers have been able to observe this arousal phenomenon in the laboratory, much remains to clarify its development and expression in relation to abuse under naturalistic circumstances.

ARE THERE DIFFERENT "TYPES" OF ABUSIVE PARENTS?

The notion of an "abusive parent" can be very misleading, for it implies that a parent possesses a cluster of traits that are stable, uniform, and easily distinguishable from parents who do not abuse their children in any manner. Psychological characteristics of abusive parents are too varied and situationally based to support such a uniform view of the parent. For example, some parents who possess many of the "predispositional" characteristics of abuse (e.g., an abusive childhood, poor anger control, limited parenting skills) may never abuse their children due to more favorable circumstances that preclude such actions (e.g., an easy-to-manage child, a supportive spouse, etc.). Likewise, there are many parents reported for child abuse who reveal few, if any, of the predispositional characteristics, yet who seem to have succumbed to the extreme pressures or demands that impinge upon them. What emerges from current studies of abusive parents, therefore, is primarily a conglomerate picture that may be too global to be of benefit to treatment providers.

Because individual abusive parents do not possess all, or even most, of the psychological characteristics reported in group studies, how do we weigh the importance of these factors, especially for making individual treatment and child-apprehension decisions? One promising alternative approach (to a single-entity view of abusive parents' psychological characteristics) involves attempts to classify the different etiological and prognostic variables associated with abusive parents into more specific subgroupings. As with any taxonomic scheme, such efforts may facilitate more precision in defining research populations and lead to more accurate etiological relationships and treatment recommendations.

Based on the early clinical reports with abusive parents (see Table 4.1), personality "typologies" were developed to improve detection of characterological differences between abusive and nonabusive parents. The earliest and most commonly cited effort at classification was proposed by Merrill (1962), who identified three distinct clusters of personality characteristics that applied to abusing mothers and fathers: (1) hostile-aggressive; (2) rigid-compulsive; and (3) passive-dependent. A fourth proposed grouping applied to fathers only, and referred to situations in which the father was out of work, frustrated, and/or responsible for child care while the mother worked. A description of these four types, along with two recently added categories, is shown in Table 4.3.

Sloan and Meier (1983) report on their attempt to classify 50 abusive parents using the six categories shown in Table 4.3. Based on clinical ratings, test findings, and diagnostic interviews, parents were assigned to one of the six groups by professional staff; however, no effort to keep the raters blind or to establish reliability of ratings was attempted in this preliminary investigation. It is interesting to note from their findings that the largest groups were the hostile-aggressive (28%) and the passive-dependent (38%). These two "types" of abusive parent groupings appear to manifest their parent-child difficulties in quite different manners (that is, very extroverted and antisocial in the former and passive, immature, and dependent on the child for emotional needs in the latter), yet both groupings represent common and difficult-to-modify patterns of abuse. In contrast, the typologies that represent the more favorable prognoses (based on therapist estimates of response to ongoing treatment) were those described as rigid-compulsive, experiencing identity or role crisis, or displaced abuse/violence. Prognoses were considerably more guarded for parents whose abusive behavior appeared to be a function of extremely maladaptive resolutions of major life crises, that is, hostile-aggressive, passive-dependent, and severe mental illness.

It is useful to relate these six child abuse typologies to the classification of parenting styles presented in Figure 2.1 (Chapter 2). Research with a full range of parenting "types" (from highly effective to deviant parent populations) has revealed only two major dimensions of parenting—demandingness and responsiveness—which intersect to

TABLE 4.3
Modified Typology for Abusive Parents

Principal Parent Characteristics	Hostile-Aggressive 1	Rigid-Compulsive 2	Passive Dependent 3
Principal dynamics	Frustrated, impulsive, and angry over childhood; extroverted; low SES and neglect.	Overly high expectations; lack of warmth and understanding; delayed child.	Immature, role reversal; identified problem child.
DSM III likelihood	Antisocial personality	Compulsive personality	Dependent personality
Abuse	Uncontrollable	Controllable	Uncontrollable, acute/severe
Proportion of 50 parents	14	3	19
Parent treatment	STEP[1]; institute impulse control; redirect hostility	STEP: nonpunitive discipline; realistic expectations	STEP: psychotherapy; home visitors; rapport easy to establish but overly dependent and resentful
Prognosis	Moderate	Good	Guarded

	Identity/Role Crisis 4	Displaced Abuse 5	Severe Mental Illness 6
Principal dynamics	Loss of job or role; displaced anger	Marital conflict; stepchild	Unpredictable; ritualistic; suspicious; project guilt/anger; delusional; emotional/sexual abuse
DSM III likelihood	—	Isolated, explosive disorder	Borderline personality; psychotic/ sadistic/masochistic/retardation
Abuse	Controllable, acute/severe	Controllable, acute/severe	Uncontrollable
Proportion of 50 parents	4	2	8
Parent treatment	STEP; impulse control; child and home management; home visitors	STEP; marital/family therapy; impulse control	Prepare for relinquishment
Prognosis	Good	Good	Extremely guarded

NOTE: Adapted with permission from *Child Abuse & Neglect*, 7, p. 446, M. P. Sloan and J. H. Meier, Typology for parents of abused children, © 1983, Pergamon Press, Ltd.
1. STEP refers to Systematic Training for Effective Parenting (Dinkmeyer & McKay, 1982).

form four distinctive styles of parenting (Maccoby & Martin, 1983). This knowledge leads to the question of whether or not further types can be differentiated by focusing more specifically on one subpopulation of parents who abuse their children.

A comparison of Figure 2.1 with Table 4.3 reveals many similarities between both approaches, suggesting that future efforts at classification of abusive parents may profit from the literature related to parenting and child development. First of all, only the first three types of abusive parenting (Table 4.3) relate specifically to *parenting dimensions,* since the remaining three types relate more prominently to issues outside of the parent-child relationship (such as loss of job, marital conflict, or severe mental illness). Within these first three types, the dimensions of responsiveness and demandingness could easily apply. The hostile-aggressive type most clearly fits the extreme form of the Authoritarian parenting style, with an emphasis upon demandingness (and long-standing interpersonal problems and conflicts). The rigid-compulsive type also falls within the definition of Authoritarian parenting, although with more emphasis upon parental lack of sensitivity and responsiveness to the child. Finally, the passive-dependent type appears to relate more closely to the Neglecting style of parenting, in which the parent is unresponsive or rejecting of the child, and fails to place age-appropriate demands on the child.

Unfortunately, over the past 25 years these rationally derived subtypes of child-abusive parents have received little empirical validation to confirm their clinical or theoretical merit, despite their intrinsic appeal and the need for unification and simplification of findings. Reasons for this lack of attention are unclear, beyond the obvious limitations of the cost and size of such an effort. Part of the cause may lie in the increasing pessimism expressed by researchers regarding the feasibility of defining "personality" dimensions of child abusers, accompanied by the upsurge of interest in behavioral approaches that traditionally have circumvented classification issues.

One promising alternative to personality-based typologies has been developed from a cluster-analysis of behavioral categories that assess differences in parenting techniques (Oldershaw, 1986). Three distinct subgroups of abusive mothers (from a sample of 73) were empirically identified on the basis of their social interactions with their preschool-aged children. The largest subgrouping, termed *emotionally detached,* was characterized by the mothers' low involvement and lack of interest in their children. These mothers exhibited flattened affect and low rates of both positive and negative behaviors toward their children. In contrast, mothers in the second identified subgrouping, termed *harsh/intrusive,* were constantly after their children to behave more appropriately. These mothers expressed a great deal of disapproval coupled with power-assertive techniques, yet they also expressed affection and approval on occasion. The third subgroup of mothers, termed *covert/hostile,* displayed extremely high rates of humiliation and ignoring, in conjunction with denial of their children's requests, negative affective tone, and very little positive behavior. Unlike the hostile/intrusive group of mothers who used physical force, commands, and threats to obtain compliance, the covert/hostile mothers used such means as humiliation and denial of affection to express their irritation and displeasure toward the child.

In concluding this topic of abusive parent typologies, we should be reminded that many of the differences between abusers and nonabusers cannot be accounted for solely on the basis of parental personality or behavioral variables. These differences are more accurately described in reference to situational events or stressful stimuli, such as: (a) stress symptoms linked to the parenting role and coping failure, (b) a learned, reciprocal pattern of aversive exchange between the parent and child, (c) negative attributions for child misbehavior, and (d) greater conditioned emotional reactivity to child-related events (Wolfe, 1985a). Accordingly, efforts to establish typologies of abusive parents could be placing too much weight (or blame) on the parent as the "cause" of the abuse, at the expense of other important, interacting factors—namely, difficult child behavior, marital and family events, and similar stressors that exceed the ability of the parent. In other words, the *weight* of parental personality factors could be relatively small in comparison to the other issues identified with child-abusive families. As discussed in Chapter 3, child abuse is the product of an interactive process that develops over time, and therefore classification systems that focus primarily on parental characteristics must be sensitive to the other critical variables that impinge upon the parent-child relationship.

The above-mentioned approaches to classification, based on either empirically or clinically derived categories, clearly merit further replication and application, because a better understanding of the differences *within* samples of abusing parents may have a dramatic impact on our assessment and treatment directions. On a more cautious note, however, generalization of these findings to all child abusers would be premature, due largely to the fact that very few male abusers have been included in these studies. For example, a large element of neglectful or avoidant parenting practices seems to emerge from each of these attempts to classify abusive parents (e.g., "passive-dependent," "emotionally detached"). This finding is congruent with national reporting data indicating that mothers are more often associated with neglect, and fathers with abuse. The possible overlap or combination of abuse and neglect in these samples of mothers may be a major factor accounting for some of these within-group differences.

5

A DEVELOPMENTAL PERSPECTIVE OF THE ABUSED CHILD

DEFINING A DEVELOPMENTAL PERSPECTIVE OF CHILDHOOD TRAUMATIZATION

Disturbance in the parent-child relationship or the family is one of the most widely implicated factors associated with children's developmental problems and psychopathology (Garmezy, 1983). For this reason, abused children in particular are believed to have a much greater than average "risk" of developing emotional and/or behavioral problems as a more longstanding consequence of parental treatment. However, the manner in which parental abuse affects the child's ongoing development is a subject of much debate and uncertainty, due primarily to the difficulty of studying such a complex phenomenon. Understanding the putative effects of child abuse (and similar forms of family victimization) requires a familiarity with the related literature on child development and psychopathology, since these areas have already established some of the critical parameters for studying the child in the context of the family.

An understanding of the abused child also has direct relevance for improving our knowledge of the abusive parent. This is largely because psychological problems that result from parental mistreatment during childhood (e.g., low trust of others, poor moral development, aggressive behavior) may readily lead to long-term, developmental impairments that persist into adulthood. For example, the dimensions of self-control, closeness and attachment to others, peer relationships, and social competence are common themes that pervade the literature on abused children, and reemerge once again as major concerns in studies of abusive adults (see reviews by Friedrich & Boriskin, 1976; Shaw-Lamphear, 1985; Toro, 1982; Wolfe, in press). Presumably, these impairments serve to regenerate the abusive cycle.

The principle that is implied by these developmental sequelae is that issues at one developmental period lay the groundwork for subsequent issues (Sroufe & Rutter, 1984). That is, the child who fails to develop interpersonal trust, receives little affection from others, and is governed by authoritarian rule—common characteristics of the abused child—has missed important socialization experiences that may interfere with adolescent and adult relationships. From the perspective of the child's psychological development, therefore, child abuse is often more than a physical misdemeanor. The physical consequences are typically over-shadowed by the associated *disruption* in the child's critical areas of development, such as attachment, self-control, and moral and social judgments. It is these disruptions and deviations in socialization practices that may be primarily responsible for emotional and behavioral problems among abused children.

In view of the above concerns, this chapter organizes our discussion of the abused child in terms of the relationship between childhood trauma and developmental outcome and the more recent literature directed specifically at the behavioral and emotional problems reported among samples of abused children (child abuse and developmental psychopathology). The problems of the abused child are fit into a developmental perspective that serves as the hypothetical link between isolated acts of abuse and acute or chronic disturbances in the child's behavior.

THE RELATIONSHIP BETWEEN CHILDHOOD TRAUMA AND DEVELOPMENTAL OUTCOME

Initial preconceptions of how abuse affects the developing child in both the short and the long term may have been overly simplistic and fatalistic. In particular, the impact of abuse on the child's development was assumed to be invariably negative and disruptive. However, similar to other forms of adversity and trauma during childhood (e.g., parental death or divorce, war, hospitalization; see Garmezy, 1983), child abuse does not appear to affect each victim in a predictable or consistent fashion (Cicchetti & Rizley, 1981). Some child victims emerge from very abusive families relatively unscathed, leading to the realization that the impact of abuse cannot always be detected in terms of its negative or undesirable influences upon the child's development. Diverse outcomes are especially understandable when positive mediators of adjustment, such as supportive relatives or the child's coping abilities, are taken into consideration.

A further complication to an understanding of the effect of abuse on the child's development is the recognition that abuse may not be a singular event that is powerful enough to override many of the other significant events occurring in the family. Physical abuse is often accompanied by major systemic influences that in all probability share the responsibility for disrupting the child's development. These influences include the more dramatic events, such as marital violence and separation of family members, as well as the mundane yet influential everyday activities that may be disturbing or maladaptive, such as impoverished parent-child interactions, few teaching opportunities, and environmental interferences. It may be premature, on the basis of the research to date, to conclude that physical abuse is the sole or even primary contributing factor to the psychological problems noted among research samples of abused children. Such problems are most likely embedded in the nature of the parent-child relationship and, sadly, the prevention of physical abuse per se may not correct the damaging effects of this relationship without additional effort being directed at the relationship itself. Thus the *unique* impact that physical abuse has on child development may be difficult to separate from other family and environmental forces, which is important to keep in mind when reviewing the following studies of abused children.

As further preparation for understanding the impact of abuse on the child we can turn to the developmental literature that has investigated how the child's early experiences and adaptation may be connected to later psychological disorders. Sroufe and Rutter (1984) outline several connections in this regard, which serve as a theoretical background for our discussion of the abused child.

These investigators emphasize that early experience may be *directly* connected to later disorders in any of three possible ways: (1) the experience leads to a disorder at the time, which then persists throughout the child's development, (2) the experience leads to bodily changes that influence later functioning, or (3) there are altered patterns of behavior at the time, which only later on begin to take the form of a disorder. In a more *indirect* manner, early experiences can affect later psychological disorders by (4) changing the family circumstances, which in time produce a disorder, (5) altering the child's sensitivities to stress or his or her coping style, which then later on "predispose" the person to disorders (or buffer against stress), (6) affecting the individual's self-concept or attitudes, which in return influence his or her response to new situations, and (7) influencing the individual's selection of environments or the availability of opportunities.

The reasons why abused children are more prone to develop behavioral and emotional disturbances than are nonabused children can be deduced from the above relationship between early experiences and subsequent mental health. Although the specific adaptational precursors of most disorders are not known, it is possible to predict later adjustment from major age-appropriate adaptive milestones, such as flexible impulse control, high self-esteem, relative absence of behavior problems, and good peer relations in preschool (Sroufe & Fleeson, 1987). It is not surprising that these developmental milestones are most often implicated in studies of abused children. While any one of the above explanations could account for the relationship between early experiences and later disorders, Sroufe and Rutter (1984) propose that a critical mechanism is the child's *adaptational failure*. A developmental perspective of psychopathology maintains that a child forms a unique "fit" with his or her environment over time, serving both to transform that environment and to be transformed by later experiences. In other words, a child's method of adapting to environmental demands at one point in time (such as avoiding an abusive caregiver) may later compromise the child's ability to form relationships with others or to be more flexible in their style of adaptation. The abused child therefore is more prone to develop psychological disorders or adjustment problems due to the powerful influence of negative early experiences that set the course for adaptational failure.

A similar example of adaptational failure among abused children is portrayed by the child's peer relationships and interpersonal development. Early experiences of trauma, poor parental attachment, and family discord associated with child abuse could lead the child to establish a pattern of avoidance with non-family members. Whereas such an adaptational style can be viewed as appropriate or understandable within the context of an abusive family, the child may have lost important opportunities for social support and buffers against stress and psychopathology.

Further clarification of this developmental perspective of psychopathology as adaptational failure emerges from the expansive literature on children's adaptation to stress and trauma. Most notably, findings derived from a diversity of investigations converge on the conclusion that *children have a significant degree of plasticity in their adaptation to stress* (see Garmezy, 1983; Langmeier & Matejcek, 1975; Rutter, 1983). That is, a remarkable number of children seem capable of adapting successfully to extremely traumatic and stressful situations. However, a prime factor in how children respond to stress (such as war, parental separation and divorce, and major life changes) is based to a large degree on the behavior of their parents or other significant adults. Such adults appear to provide a model of efficacy for the child and an ability to exert control in the midst of confusion and upheaval (Garmezy, 1983). Once again, the abused child may suffer the greatest amount of adaptational failure relative to other children from distressed families, to the extent that he or she is deprived of positive adult relationships, effective problem solving, and feelings of control or predictability. This issue of adaptational failure provides background for the conceptual under-standing of behavioral and emotional problems of abused children that follows.

CHILD ABUSE AND DEVELOPMENTAL PSYCHOPATHOLOGY

The consequences of child abuse have only recently been examined by researchers interested in the psychological, as opposed to physical, injuries to the child. This pursuit has been hampered by the multifaceted nature of abuse, which disguises or distorts the relationships among complex etiological factors. Despite these hindrances, considerable interest and effort is being directed toward understanding what it means to be the victim of abuse, especially in terms of the child's development of such crucial areas as self-esteem, self-control, and interpersonal behavior.

While recognizing the importance of children's predispositional characteristics and their effect on parental behavior, researchers have generally chosen to describe the problems shown by abused children as *resulting from abuse* rather than as independent traits of the child. It may be more accurate to define such problems in terms of a *product of interaction* between the child's emerging personality characteristics, parental treatment, and circumstantial factors (e.g., the meso- and exosystems). However, because of the major significance of the parent's role as socialization agent for the child, it is not misleading to refer to problems shown by abused children as being primarily a function of parental behavior (that is, the parent's commission of abuse and/or omission of protective factors).

Instead of focusing on particular deviant outcomes that have been noted in the child abuse literature, the following discussion emphasizes the developmental processes that are theorized to be responsible for various problems shown by abused children. This format is organized around three major dimensions of child development: (1) behavioral (e.g., aggression, poor self-control), (2) socioemotional (e.g., problems of attachment and relationship development), and (3) social-cognitive (e.g., cognitive and moral development; Smetana, Kelly, & Twentyman, 1984). The recognized importance of each dimension to child development will first be delineated, followed by the suspected manner in which abuse interferes with the normal developmental process and results in impairments to the child. Findings from recent empirical studies of abused children will be integrated into each topic.

This information on the abused child provides a basis for the position that the effects of abuse can best be understood in terms of how it *interferes* with these important dimensions of development. Such interference in turn may be manifested as a behavioral extreme along one or more of these dimensions, and is not tied to any particular behavioral expression per se. This perspective allows for a better understanding of the extremely variable (and at times, diametrically opposite) developmental outcomes reported among studies of abused children. A case description provided later in this chapter will illustrate the clinical symptomatology that is often associated with these developmental sequelae.

Behavioral Dimension: Problems of Self-Control and Aggression

One of the most significant changes that occurs during the early development of the parent-child relationship is the onset of socialization pressure, in which children must learn to inhibit disruptive behavior and engage in more socially approved behavior (Maccoby & Martin, 1983). It is probably not coincidental that this same developmental period (toddlerhood and preschool years) is when children are most likely to become the victims of abuse. Although the factors affecting the development of self-regulatory processes (such as the child's learning to control disruptive, spontaneous behavior) are not well understood, it is widely acknowledged that the child's interactions with caregivers plays a major role. Under favorable conditions, the parent provides the structure and contingencies to enable the child to develop his or her self-regulatory mechanisms, which is typically accomplished with some recognition and awareness of the child's developmental limitations and capabilities (e.g., as they pertain to toilet training). It is also relatively clear that the parent and child shape one another throughout this process of developing self-regulation—that is, the child's behavior is controlled not only by explicit instructions from the parent, but by his or her acquired understanding of what is allowed and what is forbidden.

As noted above, parenting methods are highly implicated in the shaping of the child's self-regulation of daily activity. More specifically, we are also interested in how children learn to develop *self-control,* which refers to a more advanced ability to engage in a behavior that may involve immediately unpleasant consequences but long-range pleasant outcomes (such as delaying gratification or inhibiting aggression; Harter, 1983). In this respect, parental methods of *punishment* play an important role in the emergence of self-control in children. Aronfreed (1968), for example, has emphasized the role of punishment in bringing about the child's internalized control over behavior. The child's affective state (e.g., anxiety, guilt, shame) may become conditioned to mental representations of events that are contiguous with the occurrence of punishment. In other words, children associate feelings of fear, shame, or anxiety with their behavior, and thus learn to suppress such transgressions in the future. Moreover, punishments appear to be most effective if they are accompanied by an explicit rationale, especially one based on empathy or an appreciation of others (see Harter, 1983).

Because the importance of effective punishment is underscored by these findings, important distinctions should be made between appropriate and inappropriate administration of punishment. The bulk of evidence indicates that an overreliance on power-assertive, extrapunitive parenting methods is associated with elevated rates of aggressive behavior (i.e., low self-control) in children, especially if such punishment is delivered in an inconsistent manner (see Maccoby & Martin, 1983; Parke & Slaby, 1983). Studies of aggressive families (e.g., Patterson, 1982) have shown that such family members are more likely to prolong or escalate a mildly aversive encounter into a serious fight. Instead of responding to the child's misbehavior with a level and form of punishment that is commensurate with the child's misdeed, the parents of aggressive children use weak or ineffective punishments initially and are thus required to respond with further force when the child fails to respond. This pattern seems to perpetuate the use of coercion between family members, and further impairs the child's development of self-control.

It is this coercive process that may be operative in abusive families as well: Parental punishment is delivered in a fashion that fails to teach the child to inhibit or control his or her behavior, and thus the parents fail to provide the child with further assistance in learning self-control. The parent responds to the child only when his or her level of tolerance is exceeded (i.e., punishes the child "in anger"), rather than in response to the child's need to learn appropriate behavior. Such delay in applying punishment reduces its effectiveness, and may also necessitate a stronger (and less cautious) response when the child continues the misconduct. Moreover, a rationale for punishment is seldom provided by the parent in a manner that the child can comprehend. These propositions are supported by the following studies of abused children.

Behavior Problems Among Abused Children

Aggression. The theme of aggressive behavior and poor self-control continues throughout the development of abused children, providing empirical support for the contentions just described (although it should be recognized that not all abused children behave in this fashion). Studies of social behavior with peers and adults have found that, beginning with preschool age, abused children direct significantly more aggression toward peers (Egeland & Sroufe, 1981; George & Main, 1979; Hoffman-Plotkin & Twentyman, 1984; Reidy, 1977; Sangrund, Gaines, & Green, 1974). These young children also are found to exhibit a complex array of social behaviors indicative of poor self-control, distractability, and negative emotion, such as low enthusiasm and resistance to directions (Gaensbauer & Sands, 1979).

By the time abused children reach school age, problems with aggression and peer relationships are widely reported both at home and at school. Based on observations of abused children in their homes, several studies have reported that the children exhibit high rates of aggressive and aversive behaviors, such as hitting, yelling, and destructiveness when interacting with parents or siblings (Bousha & Twentyman, 1984; Lahey et al., 1984; Lorber et al., 1984; Reid et al., 1981). For example, Lahey et al. (1984) reported that an average of 4% of the behaviors emitted by the abused children in their sample involved pushing, hitting, or grabbing, as compared with 1.5% of children from low-income families and 0.5% from middle-income families. These behavior patterns resemble those often displayed by children with behavior problems from distressed families, which recalls the link between parental treatment and child behavior problems noted above.

Social competence. The preschool- and school-aged abused child, moreover, is often *perceived* by teachers and parents as being more difficult to manage, less socially mature, and less capable of developing trust with others (Herrenkohl, Herrenkohl, Toedter, & Yanushefski, 1984; Kinard, 1980; Salzinger, Kaplan, Pelcovitz, Samit, & Kreiger, 1984; Wolfe & Mosk, 1983). It comes as no surprise, therefore, that abused children often have poor peer relationships marked by rejection or neglect, presumably in response to the child's deficits in social skills (e.g., Perry, Doran, & Wells, 1983), lowered social competence (Wolfe & Mosk, 1983), and less social involvement with their peers (Mash et al., 1983).

Violence and juvenile crime. The behavioral consequences of abuse have until recently been limited primarily to short-term effects assessed within one year following the abuse report. Yet a major fear expressed in the literature and public media is that the association between child abuse and aggressive behavior (as noted above) will predispose the child over time to become antisocial or violent. This association makes intuitive sense, due to the child's exposure to a lifelong history of interpersonal violence in which power assertion and dominance may be easily adopted. Studies have recently emerged to support this relationship, although conclusions must be cautiously drawn until further improvements in design have been made.

In particular, the greatest source of support for the association between abuse during childhood and violent and antisocial behavior during adolescence is derived from samples of delinquent populations. Several authors have noted that the most striking factor distinguishing violent from nonviolent delinquents is the amount of violence in the adolescent's past (Lewis et al., 1979; Loeber, Weisman, & Reid, 1983; Tarter et al., 1984). For example, when Tarter et al. (1984) dichotomized the crimes of delinquents referred by juvenile court as assaultive or nonassaultive, they discovered that 44% of the abused delinquents (N = 27) committed violent crimes, in comparison to 16% (N = 74) of the nonabused delinquents. Related findings were reported in a 40-year longitudinal study of 232 males from violent and nonviolent low-income families (McCord, 1979, 1983). The author found that 22% of the abused (N = 49), 23% of the neglected (N = 48), and 50% of the rejected (N = 34) boys had been later convicted for serious juvenile crimes, such as theft, auto theft, burglary, or assault, compared to 11% (N = 101) of the boys from matched comparison families.

To recapitulate, indiscriminate, inconsistent, and power-assertive parenting practices are believed to interfere with children's development of self-control and to increase their resistance to control exerted by disciplinary agents such as parents and teachers. Poor self-control, in return, is associated with children's increased aggressiveness and lowered social competence in peer relationships. Recent studies of abused children illustrate this relationship quite clearly. Some of these children have learned (presumably through early experiences of parental modeling of aggression and use of ineffective punishment) to use aggressive behavior as a legitimate or predominant means of resolving interpersonal conflicts.

Socioemotional Dimension: Deficits in
Social Sensitivity and Relationship Development

In addition to the development of self-control, early experiences with the caregiver are very important in terms of the child's development of positive relationships with others and contentment in his or her social environment. The quality of infant-caregiver attachment, in particular, is believed to be the product of characteristic styles of mutual interaction over the first year of life, involving such parental characteristics as sensitivity and responsiveness to the infant's needs and signals (Ainsworth, 1980). Lipsitt (1983) views such parent-child attachment as a form of "stress reducer" for the child. That is, the period of infancy provides rehearsal and practice for later defense against many of the stressful environmental factors with which the child must learn to cope. Thus the attachment period, in a manner of speaking, represents a stressful process involving a "tug-of-war" between the infant's needs and claims and the caregiver's desire for reciprocity from the infant (Lipsett, 1983).

The security or quality of the early relationship formation between the parent and the child has been linked to the child's emerging mastery of the social and physical environment. Thus secure attachment promotes a high level of capabilities, goals, and actions throughout development (Schneider-Rosen & Cicchetti, 1984). In contrast, poor attachment formation during early childhood may predispose a child to increased risk of psychopathology later in life. This latter hypothesis was tested in a longitudinal study by Lewis, Feiring, McGuffog, and Jaskir (1984), in which 113 children were seen at one and six years of age to examine the relationship between early attachment and later psychopathology. For boys, attachment classification (that is, securely or insecurely attached) was significantly related to psychopathology: Insecurely attached males showed significant elevations on the Child Behavior Profile (Achenbach & Edelbrock, 1981), whereas securely attached males did not. It is interesting that no relationship was found for the females in the study, an issue that merits further investigation. The authors note that although 40% of the insecurely attached males showed later signs of adjustment problems, the remaining 60% who had shown insecure attachment *did not* reveal later psychopathological symptoms. This finding reaffirms an important issue in developmental psychopathology: Early experiences may *predispose* a child to subsequent psychopathology, especially in the presence of stress factors. Infants are neither made invulnerable by secure attachments nor are they doomed by insecure attachments to later adjustment disorders.

Sroufe and Fleeson (1987) make an intriguing argument that relates the child's early attachment experiences to his or her relationship history. Drawing upon the well-accepted attachment literature, they make the claim that early relationships shape what the child knows how to do and what he or she understands. Thus if the child has known hostile, punitive relationships with adults, this is what he or she comes to expect or even to rely on. These relationship histories presumably are carried forward over generations through the process of coherence, in which the individual continues or reestablishes relationships that are congruent with his or her past relationship experience. According to this argument, relationship patterns are learned merely by being in relationships and, once established, seem especially difficult to change. This viewpoint is germane to the experiences of abused children, who may form future relationships that are shaped in part by their inappropriate knowledge of sex-role expectations, power assertion, emotional rejection, or other possible components that interfere with the establishment of positive, supportive relationships.

Disturbances in Relationship Development and Affect Among Abused Children

Researchers have been interested in how the developing parent-child relationship may be affected under the adverse conditions of emotional rejection, harsh treatment, insensitivity, and verbal and physical assaults (Aber & Cicchetti, 1984; Ainsworth, 1980). Two approaches to understanding the socioemotional development of abused children have been predominant: (a) investigations of attachment formation with infants and toddlers, and (b) studies of preschool- and school-aged abused children's ability to empathize with their peers and to form positive peer relationships. A third area, disturbance of affect, is also emerging as an important area of investigation. Each of these topics will be examined separately.

Attachment formation. A strong consensus has been formed, based on comparative and prospective studies, in support of the conclusion that child abuse during infancy and early childhood is associated with insecure attachment relationships with the caregiver (e.g., Crittenden, 1985; Dietrich et al., 1980; Egeland & Sroufe, 1981; Egeland & Vaughn, 1981; Schneider-Rosen & Cicchetti, 1984). When observed in the "strange situation" (an unfamiliar task whereby the infant's behavior is studied in relation to the presence or absence of the mother), abused infants have been found to cling to their mothers and/or display negative affect toward their caregivers significantly more often than nonabused controls. When studied longitudinally, those abused children showing early attachment problems were more likely to reveal declining developmental abilities over the first two years of life, especially in critical areas of speech, language, and social interaction (Egeland & Farber, 1984; Egeland & Sroufe, 1981). The importance of the early parent-child relationship is thus underscored by these findings, especially since they may represent the possible beginnings of parent-child conflict, parental nonresponsiveness to infant demands, parental failure to provide stimulation and comfort, and infant characteristics that interact with parental ability.

Problems in attachment have led to a great deal of speculation regarding perinatal risk factors that may increase the likelihood of child abuse. That is, children who are born with certain congenital characteristics (e.g., low birth weight, prematurity, mental retardation, unusual physical appearance or anomalies, handicaps) may be less acceptable or less satisfying to a parent, thereby increasing stress upon the parent. However, what has emerged from studies of this relationship is a less obvious association between handicapping conditions and abuse. Starr (1982) found, for example, that minor deviations in child behavior (e.g., poor motor coordination, slow language development, being less affectionate), rather than the major handicaps noted above, were most often related to the occurrence of abuse in his large sample. This somewhat paradoxical conclusion makes greater sense in light of the possibility that parents of a noticeably handicapped child may often attribute behavioral problems to the handicap itself, whereas parents with infants who appear physically normal but who show subtle deviations in behavior and development may be more likely to attribute problems to things that the child can control, leading to parental reactions that blame the child and increase punitive controls.

Empathy and social sensitivity. As abused children grow older they are faced with another very important period of relationship development, this time with peers and other adults. During preschool and school ages, therefore, child abuse researchers center their interest on the children's initial manifestations of sensitivity to others' emotions and their early prosocial behavior. A positive bond or relationship between parent and child is considered to be an important component of such development among nonabused children, and therefore one would expect that abused children would show problems in their understanding or acceptance of the emotions of others. This area of research has been a particularly difficult one in which to establish firm relationships, since a number of individual, parental, familial, and cultural factors influence the expression of empathy and prosocial behavior (Radke-Yarrow, Zahn-Waxler, & Chapman, 1983).

Despite these complications, initial studies indicated that abused children performed more poorly than nonabused controls on measures of affective and cognitive role-taking, social sensitivity, and the ability to discriminate emotions in others (Barahal, Waterman, & Martin, 1981; Frodi & Smetana, 1984; Straker & Jacobson, 1981). These results are illustrated by the findings of a recent study involving 10 abused and 10 nonabused toddlers matched on a number of sociodemographic and disadvantage variables (Main & George, 1985). No abused child ever exhibited a concerned response at witnessing the distress (e.g., crying, fearful) of another toddler, whereas the nonabused children responded with a concerned expression to one-third of the distress events. Furthermore, the abused children not only failed to show concern, they actively responded to distress in others with *fear, physical attack, or anger.* Thus abused children appear to bear a strong behavioral resemblance to their own abusive parents regarding their tendency to isolate themselves, to respond aggressively under a range of circumstances, and to respond with anger and aversion to the distress of others (Main & George, 1985).

Affect disturbance. The above studies have addressed the socioemotional development of abused children by focusing on deficits in their ability to develop supportive, nonaggressive relationships with others. This approach has led to a better understanding of the link between problems in the parent-child relationship and subsequent interpersonal adjustment. However, very little attention has been given to understanding the emotional symptoms or disorders that might be expected on the basis of their early experiences (see Kinard, 1982).

To address this concern, Kazdin, Moser, Colbus, and Bell (1985) studied depressive symptoms among abused (N = 33) and psychiatrically disturbed latency-aged children (N = 46) in an inpatient setting. Their focus on depressive symptoms (e.g., impaired ability to enjoy life, sad affect, low self-esteem, social withdrawal) was derived from concerns expressed in clinical reports, as well as the suspected relationship between the use of harsh punishment and the development of learned helplessness (i.e., feelings of low control over aversive events). Moreover, the lack of affection, emotional rejection, and social isolation shown by abusive parents was believed to contribute to the child's risk of affect disorder.

These investigators found significantly higher levels of self-reported depression and hopelessness and lower self-esteem among the abused than the nonabused child patients (while controlling for major sociodemographic variables as well as the child's overall level of distress or severity of psychopathology). Furthermore, children with both *past and current abuse* were the most severely depressed, suggesting to the authors that "a history of abuse retains its impact on the child and augments the effect of current abuse" (1985, p. 305). This study highlights the *emotional trauma* that may be experienced by the child in relation to abusive child-rearing practices, leading to overt or covert emotional and behavioral symptomatology. Such trauma may be a significant component affecting the child's development in a number of important areas, discussed later in this chapter.

Social-Cognitive Dimension:
Issues in Cognitive and Moral Development

Social-cognitive development is a third area in which parent-child reciprocation appears to foster the child's mature functioning. Parents who exercise firm control (in the sense of following through on their demands), while at the same time exhibiting warmth and nurturance to their children, are more likely to have children who behave in a prosocial manner and who are concerned with the effects of their behavior on others (Hoffman, 1970; Radke-Yarrow et al., 1983). In contrast, studies attempting to predict children's display of "conscience" or "guilt" find that power-assertive (i.e., authoritarian) child-rearing techniques are those that are most often associated with low scores on measures of children's conscience (see Hoffman, 1970).

This association between children's moral development and parenting practices has led researchers to investigate the methods of reasoning or explanations parents use that are most conducive to *internalization* in children—that is, children's ability to regulate their own behavior in a manner that is sensitive to the rights of others, and that originates from their own intention, rather than from fear of punishment or hope of reward (Maccoby & Martin, 1983). Children who develop an inner locus of control and positive self-esteem are more likely to succeed in future pursuits such as schoolwork, peer activities, and athletic accomplishments. Maccoby and Martin (1983) review the results of several decades of research on the content of parent-child communication that influences the child's development of conscience and prosocial behavior, concluding that

> a certain amount of moral exhortation on the part of parents does seem to have some effect. At least, repeated parental stress on the consequences (especially consequences for others) of children's actions seems to move them toward more mature levels of thought when they are asked to consider moral issues. (p. 53)

Thus if a parent wishes to have the child behave in a certain manner in situations where the parent is not present, moral explanations that refer to the effects on others need to be invoked.

Parental teaching methods that rely on coercion and authority may interfere as well with developmental processes other than moral and social judgment. Such methods may also limit the child's intellectual curiosity and advancement, which become manifest during early school years. We know from studies of nonabused children that high levels of parental demandingness and responsivity (the Authoritative parenting style) are often associated with higher social assertiveness, social responsibility, and cognitive competence in children (e.g., Baumrind & Black, 1967). *Ipso facto,* parents who are unresponsive to their children's intellectual, social, and emotional signals and abilities while placing high demands and expectations upon them are more likely to interfere with their children's acquisition of necessary skills for the academic setting, such as their motivation to learn, their willingness to follow directions, and their self-control of disruptive and inappropriate behavior with peers.

Problems in Social Judgment and School Performance Among Abused Children

Because abused children have been raised in an atmosphere of power-assertion and external control, it is suspected that their level of moral reasoning would be significantly below their nonabused peers. Typically, abusive parents fail to invoke in their children concern for the welfare of others, especially in a manner that the child will internalize and imitate. From a developmental-psychopathological viewpoint, therefore, it is important to determine whether abused children differ from other children in their conceptions of the permissibility of moral transgressions, such as the acceptability of physical or psychological distress in others, or the unfair distribution of resources (Smetana et al., 1984). Such findings could help to explain why abused children behave more aggressively toward their peers, through their adherence to a self- as opposed to other-centered value system. This topic has been explored only recently with abused children and the preliminary findings are reviewed below, followed by problems related to school performance and intellectual ability.

Social and moral judgment. Judgments regarding different types of moral transgressions have been systematically examined with abused children in only one well-designed study to date (Smetana et al., 1984). The findings from this study will be discussed in some detail, in anticipation of further work being conducted in this area.

These investigators compared 12 abused, 16 neglected, and 16 matched control children of preschool age in their judgments regarding the dimensions of seriousness, deserved punishment, rule contingency (the permissibility of actions in the absence of rules), and generalizability of familiar moral and conventional nursery school transgressions. These moral transgressions included pictures depicting physical harm (hitting, kicking, biting), psychological distress (making another child cry, teasing, being mean to another child), and resource distribution (taking away another child's snack, not taking turns with a toy). Social-conventional transgressions involved pictures indicating not listening to the teacher during story time, not keeping quiet during nap time, and leaving the classroom without permission. Children were individually shown these pictures to obtain ratings of their judgments in reference to the four dimensions noted above.

The results distinguished primarily between the two *maltreated* groups of abused and neglected children. Abused children considered transgressions entailing psychological distress to be more universally wrong for others (but not for themselves), whereas neglected children considered the unfair distribution of resources to be more universally wrong for themselves (but not for others). These findings are consistent with the type of maltreatment experienced by each of the two groups of children. It appears that abused children, as a function of their physical and psychological maltreatment, may have a heightened sensitivity to the intrinsic wrongness of such offenses. However, further clarification is needed to understand the somewhat paradoxical relationship between this increased sensitivity and higher rates of aggression that are observed among abused children. We know from related studies of children's attributions that children who are described as aggressive (in contrast to nonaggressive children) attribute hostile intent in the face of ambiguous provocations directed at them (Dodge & Frame, 1982), and socially rejected or neglected children tend to perceive *prosocial* intentions of their peers as being hostile (Dodge, Murphy, & Buchsbaum, 1984). Further awareness of children's *perceptions* of their peers' intentions therefore may advance our understanding of the relationship between children's thoughts and behavior, especially in the aftermath of abusive treatment at home.

Smetana et al. (1984) conclude on the basis of their study that, with intelligence and social class controlled, abused and neglected children differ from nonmaltreated children in moral and social-conventional judgments that seem to be closely related to their experiences of maltreatment. This finding is consistent with the assertion that children's moral and social judgments are actively constructed from social experiences that, in this case, may have involved the internalization of standards of behavior that reflect their own victimization experiences.

Academic performance. From preschool age and beyond, studies have found that abused children are significantly more likely than their peers to show delays related to cognitive development. Such delays are typically attributed to the limited stimulation received in the home by parents who are overly concerned with the child's behavioral appearance and obedience, to the detriment of the child's need to explore, attempt new challenges, and to be exposed to a variety of cognitive and social stimuli. Along these same lines, punishment that involves verbal, emotional, and/or physical abuse is likely to have a suppressing effect upon many aspects of the child's interpersonal behavior (Parke & Slaby, 1983), which may partially account for the child's slowness in acquiring new cognitive and social skills. Child abuse, therefore, is a double-edged sword that may exacerbate many of the developmental lags or problems that the parent intended to rectify.

This assertion is borne out by studies revealing significant deficits in abused children's academic performance and intellectual functioning (Applebaum, 1977; Barahal et al., 1981; Friedrich, Einbender, & Lueke, 1983; Hoffman-Plotkin & Twentyman, 1984; Sandgrund et al., 1974). For example, an average difference of approximately 20 IQ points was revealed in a comparison of abused and nonabused preschoolers on the Stanford Binet Intelligence Scale and the Peabody Picture Vocabulary Test (Hoffman-Plotkin & Twentyman, 1984). Similar concerns emerge among school-aged samples of abused children. Salzinger et al. (1984) compared 30 abused children with 26 neglected and 48 nonmaltreated children on standard achievement tests and measures of classroom performance. Both the abused and neglected groups of children were two years below grade level in verbal abilities (27% for maltreated group versus 9% for controls) and math abilities (33% versus 3%). As well, approximately one-third of the abused and neglected samples were failing one or more subjects and/or placed in a special classroom. It is interesting to note from this study of classroom performance that not only the children who had been targets of maltreatment performed poorly at school; their siblings (who were an average of two years older) were at comparably below-average levels of academic performance.

The above findings point to the need to assess the consequences of physical abuse (and concomitant maltreatment) in relation to the child's developmental pace and relative deficits. Once such children become involved in the school system, impairments in cognitive, social, and emotional development *that may have originated from deficits in the parent-child relationship* can readily interfere with school performance and peer adjustment and become mislabeled as problems stemming from the child's motivation, intelligence, physiology, and so on. Although the remediation of such developmental problems may rely heavily upon social interventions involving the school and community, we should keep in mind the importance of the quality of the parent-child relationship in determining the child's future adjustment, and act accordingly to assist the child in gaining these skills.

A Clinical Illustration

It has been shown throughout this chapter that children's reactions to chronic abuse and the accompanying family dysfunction can vary considerably, ranging from symptoms that are barely detectable to reactions that are quite dramatic and severe. Incidents of child abuse seldom bear a linear relationship to child development, in that many individual, social, and environmental variables can modulate the impact of abuse on the child. Yet the *emotional* trauma that almost inevitably accompanies episodes of physical abuse and other forms of family victimization can play a demonstrative role in affecting the child's reactions to harsh parental treatment. The child's extreme emotional reactions, in return, may be misattributed by the parent (as well as child-care professionals who are unaware of the abuse) as due to the child's escalating defiance, beguilement, or disturbance, prompting further mistreatment.

This malignant pattern may have very severe consequences for the child, as illustrated by the case of Jimmy, a 3½-year-old victim of physical and emotional abuse. Jimmy was hospitalized three times over a four-month period (beginning at age 3) for symptoms of dehydration, failure to thrive, and a coma resulting from the ingestion of motor oil (which he had found in a garbage dumpster). The hospital initially had diagnosed his physical problems (prior to the motor oil incident) as being related to a common bacterial infection that impaired his digestion. His diagnosis following his third admission was pica (a morbid appetite for unusual or unfit food), and he was assessed in a number of physical and psychological areas to determine the possible origins of such behavior. The results of such testing revealed an average intellectual functioning, normal sensory-motor development, and no detectable physical basis for his behavior.

Jimmy's mother (with whom he had lived alone since birth) reported that his behavior at home was difficult at times but manageable, with only occasional bed-wetting and noncompliance. He was not known to be an accident-prone or overactive child. The only changes that had recently occurred in his life involved his mother's boyfriend moving into the home and participating in child care. Jimmy had also visited his birth father prior to the onset of the physical symptoms.

Following his third return home from the hospital, Jimmy's mother reported to the social worker (who was assigned to the family following the hospitalizations) that he was becoming more resistant to her attempts to discipline him, and that he was urinating on his pillow, bed, the rug, and on doors. She further stated that Jimmy was making himself vomit, and he would ingest or place in his mouth a variety of filthy objects. The origin of these behavior problems was unknown, and was assumed at first to be a function of the mother's limited parenting experience, since she had been abused as a child and was known to the social agency since her childhood. However, it was later discovered by the social worker that, because of the worsening behavior problems, the mother and her boyfriend had set up independent living quarters for Jimmy in the basement, equipped with a table and chairs, a cot, an air mattress, and blankets. He slept in these basement quarters for an estimated two or three months before this came to the attention of the social worker, since he was allowed to socialize with the family during the daytime.

This discovery led to the removal of Jimmy from his mother and his placement into a foster home. In this new setting, Jimmy's pica never recurred and he was described in positive terms by the foster parents. A fuller understanding of Jimmy's emotional disturbance then began to emerge within three weeks of placement in the foster home. He began to refer to mother's boyfriend as a "bad guy," and described to the foster parents and social worker several abusive episodes in which the boyfriend had sprayed him in the face with a hose, kicked his ankle, flicked him in the eyes with his fingers, hit him on the head, and frightened him by putting him in the basement. The ensuing investigation revealed that these episodes had indeed occurred. Jimmy's mother acknowledged that she had witnessed some of the abuse, and eventually told her boyfriend to leave the home. She explained that in her desperation to resolve some of Jimmy's earlier problems with bed-wetting and so on, she had taken her boyfriend's advice and allowed Jimmy to be isolated from the family and mistreated.

CHILD ABUSE AS VICTIMIZATION:
A CLOSER LOOK AT THE EMOTIONAL IMPACT OF ABUSE

In attempting to understand the diverse impact that abuse may have on child development, we have reviewed studies that have implicated physical abuse as a significant factor related to disturbances in the child's observable behavior. Several studies have speculated on the psychological processes underlying these behavioral differences shown by abused children, especially in terms of children's behavioral, socioemotional, and social-cognitive development. These processes notably include young infants' emotional attachment to caregivers, children's cognitive formation of moral judgments and empathy, and self-control based on parental modeling and child-rearing techniques.

In this last section, we will explore an additional mechanism that also may be responsible for the emotional and behavioral disturbances shown among abused children—the emotional trauma resulting from chronic rejection, loss of affection, betrayal, and feelings of helplessness that may accompany chronic mistreatment by one's own family members. This emotional trauma has been referred to as *victimization* in reference to adult populations (e.g., victims of rape, incest, crime, and so on). In the present context of child development, the term *family victimization* will be used to denote the dilemma faced by abused children: How to compensate for the absence of affection, consistency, attention, and similar emotional needs that are typically provided by family members.

One persistent question that cannot be directly answered through observations of abused children is, How does abuse during childhood affect children's developing view of the world and themselves? The victims' lingering negative evaluations of themselves, their families, and the world in general is of primary interest since their future behavior may be largely affected by such viewpoints. Approaching this issue in reference to adult victims of personal crimes, Peterson and Seligman (1983) describe how the learned helplessness model and its reformulation might aid in understanding reactions to victimization that involve what they term "emotional numbing and maladaptive passivity" (p. 103). They propose that during traumatic episodes involving personal danger (such as abusive incidents) a response by the victim is futile. Such experiences in turn can result in learning an expectation of future helplessness, whereby the victim comes to believe that there is little that he or she can do to prevent or gain control over stressful situations. The result is the development of a passive response style in new situations that may be unrelated to the one that was originally encountered. Dialogues with victims of violent crimes support this contention of learned helplessness, indicating that many victims express feelings of self-doubt, insecurity, elevated fears, and anxiety across a diversity of situations (Kilpatrick, Best, & Veronen, 1978; Veronen & Kilpatrick, 1980).

The individual differences shown in response to stressful events (e.g., aggression, passivity, self-blame) are accounted for by the revised learned helplessness model (Abramson, Seligman, & Teasdale, 1978) in reference to three dimensions of causal attributions about uncontrolled events: internal-external, stable-unstable, and global-specific. An abused child, according to this reasoning, may learn to attribute stressful, uncontrollable events to something about himself or herself (internal attribution), as opposed to something about the situation or circumstances (external), which makes the child more prone to a loss of self-esteem. Similarly, if the child perceives the cause to be persistent across time (stable) versus transient (unstable), then he or she is more prone to *chronic* helplessness. Finally, if the child comes to believe that the cause of the event is one that will affect many areas of his or her life (global), as opposed to a single area (specific), that child may be more prone to *pervasive* deficits.

The value of the attributional perspective in understanding the plight of child abuse victims has been demonstrated in several studies of adults who were *sexually abused* during their childhood (see Browne & Finkelhor, 1986; Wolfe & Wolfe, in press). For example, Tsai, Feldman-Summers, & Edgar (1979) studied variables that were related to the differential impact on later psychological functioning of adult women who were sexually abused as children. They found that women who reported most maladjustment also reported having stronger negative feelings at the time of the sexual abuse. These women were also older when the abuse began and experienced a higher frequency and longer duration of maltreatment. The researchers concluded that differences in later adjustment could be mediated by the *emotional responses* evoked at the time of abuse, such as fear, panic, and apprehension. Such emotional reactions at the time of the traumatic event favor the development of conditioned emotional responses that may recur incessantly in the presence of eliciting stimuli, such as a picture of the person, reminders of the circumstances, or proximity to the place where the event occurred. Evidence for such recurrent discomfort and traumatization (e.g., nightmares, phobias, oversensitivity toward others) can be found in numerous studies of adult victims of violent crimes (see Janoff-Bulman & Frieze, 1983; Veronen & Kilpatrick, 1980).

Silver, Boon, and Stones (1983) similarly studied women with past incestuous experiences in childhood, asking them to what degree they had resolved their feelings about the incest (e.g., "How did you deal with the experience?"; "How did you come to accept it?"). Individuals described as "searching for meaning" (i.e., those who could not attribute the abuse to explainable circumstances) tended to be more plagued by intrusive thoughts about the experiences that interfered with their daily activity. On a more positive note, however, this latter study identified the importance of close social relationships and supports in further moderating the impact of victimization experiences.

A similar process involving conditioned emotional responses and attributions for traumatic events may be operative with children who are physically abused by their caregivers. Such processes, moreover, may help to explain the somewhat peculiar and unpredictable adjustment reactions sometimes shown by abused children and adolescents, such as hoarding food, self-injurious behavior, urinating on personal belongings, and hurting other children (see Green, 1983; Wolfe, in press). The emotional reactions that are elicited by harsh and abusive punishment require the child to "search for meaning" for such treatment, especially since these negative feelings are the result of behavior by *significant members of the child's own family*. Rather than acknowledge or believe that one's own parents could be at fault, some abused children may shift the blame to persons or circumstances that they find more acceptable (such as situational factors or external events that are less important than one's own parents). This personal viewpoint of the situation may then function as the child's explanation and justification to others for his or her family problems and resultant disruption.

In some instances (such as when the family is reunited and abuse is terminated), children's tendency to place blame for family disruption on less significant persons or events (e.g., teachers, parents' employers, siblings) may serve as a "self-protection mechanism" that allows them to maintain a more positive or acceptable view of their parents, *even if such a view may not be entirely accurate*. A less favorable outcome, from the perspective of children's development, may result if abused children attribute their emotional discomfort and pain to their own fallibilities (e.g., "I'm a bad person who brings trouble to my family") or to global events that are not amenable to change (e.g., "These things happen to a lot of children;""There's little I can do to prevent such things from happening in the future"). It has long been suggested, as well, that children who misattribute their harsh treatment at home to global, nonspecific events in their environment (e.g., "The world is a dangerous place") or blame their parents for most of their misfortune are at greater risk of involvement in future aggressive acts against persons and property (Parke & Slaby, 1983). The attribution of intentionality, in particular, may be a critical determinant of dispositional inferences regarding one's abusive parents. As children grow older, such inferences regarding another person's intentions for behaving aggressively are known to become more stable and less resistant to change (e.g., Rotenberg, 1980).

One exemplary study on the topic of victims' self-reported experiences and attributions has appeared involving physically abused adolescents. Herzberger, Potts, and Dillon (1981) were interested in determining whether abused children develop distorted or maladaptive perceptions of parental characteristics, discipline techniques, and emotional acceptance or rejection that affect their subsequent adjustment and behavior. The researchers conducted individual interviews with 14 boys between 8 and 14 years of age who had been previously abused and were living in a residential group home. These children had been removed from their abusive parents for an average of 2.5 years, which allowed for some time to develop a personal viewpoint on their prior experiences. Responses of the 14 abused boys were compared to those of 10 boys living in the same group home for reasons other than child abuse. As predicted, the study found that abused children described their abusive parent in more negative terms and generally believed their prior treatment to be more emotionally rejecting than the boys in the control sample. When asked whether or not their parent cared about them, gave them a great deal of love, and liked having them around, the abused boys were more inclined to disagree. Of interest is the finding that there was a wide degree of variability in the abused children's perceptions of their parents and their previous mistreatment, with some of the children believing that such behavior was acceptable and deserved!

On the basis of these interviews with abuse victims, the authors draw an important distinction between those who saw their abuse as an indication of *parental rejection* and those who perceived the abuse as being caused by external events imposed on the parent (e.g., child's difficult behavior, job stress, etc.). Boys who felt their parents were rejecting, uninterested, and extrapunitive were significantly less likely to justify the abusive behavior of their parents, and generally expressed disdain toward their family. On the other hand, those who regarded the abuse as due to circumstances beyond their parents' control held more positive viewpoints of their family and seemed less bothered by the aftermath of events (e.g., moving to a group home). As stated previously, whether or not this latter attributional perspective is accurate in terms of the reasons for abusive treatment does not seem to be as significant as the child's personal construction of events. Some severely mistreated children ostensibly could show fewer signs of maladjustment than less severely mistreated children, based on the manner in which they subsequently come to view the reasons for their mistreatment and their emotional discomfort.

CONCLUSIONS

This chapter has discussed the circuitous and unpredictable manner in which child maltreatment is believed to affect children's behavioral and emotional expression, as well as their cognitive view of the world. Overall, the nonspecific signs and symptoms of *developmental deviation* or peculiarity appear to be indicative of the child's trauma rather than the presence of a recognizable pattern of symptoms per se. As shown by recent studies, the most common developmental deviations relate to aggressive and noncompliant behavior, poor peer relationships, insecure attachment, impaired moral development, and general symptoms of anxiety and insecurity. However, a child who is subjected to abusive treatment can potentially react in any of a number of ways, including serious displays of self-injurious behavior, as shown in the clinical illustration of a 3½-year-old abused boy.

In conjunction with the developmental perspective of the abused child, the importance of viewing child abuse as "family victimization" has been raised herein to broaden our view of the plight of abuse victims. Victimization encompasses a number of psychological processes that may potentially interfere with healthy development and lead to the perpetuation of abuse across generations. The most significant of these processes was defined in relation to the child's social-cognitive development, or how he or she comes to view how the world operates. This victimization concept helps to underscore the importance of the *emotional* components of physical abuse, which are frequently absent or implicitly contained in discussions of the impact of abuse on the child. This argument rests in part on the presumed importance of the family as the child's major socialization arena, thereby creating feelings of betrayal, confusion, rejection, and similar emotional reactions on the part of the child as a consequence of abusive treatment from family members. Such a relationship between family victimization during childhood and subsequent adjustment problems during adulthood has been supported by recent studies of sexually and physically abused children. Insights obtained from these related investigations may bridge some of the gap in understanding the emotional, as well as behavioral, impact of child abuse.

6

IMPLICATIONS FOR PREVENTION AND EARLY INTERVENTION

Throughout this book child abuse has been described in relation to socialization practices that have a pervasive impact on child development. Most forms of physical abuse entail many of the actions and circumstances that are indicative of socialization failure. A critical need exists to discover different ways of preventing such failure well in advance of the establishment of abusive and rejecting patterns of child rearing. This prevention task is now a distinct possibility in view of our acquired knowledge of the social and psychological causes of child abuse. For example, the causes of certain types of abuse, especially abuse of young, preschool-aged children, have been fairly well documented over the past decade through research efforts. Based on this knowledge foundation, a top priority exists to formulate, implement, and evaluate the effectiveness of prevention-oriented programs for child abuse.

The urgency to develop effective prevention strategies for abuse, both at a primary and a secondary level, has been clearly expressed (see Alvy, 1975; Rosenberg & Reppucci, 1985; Williams, 1983; Wolfe, 1985b). This prevention orientation reflects the skepticism and frustration of many researchers and clinicians who find it difficult to modify abusive socialization practices that have been in effect. Over time, family members anticipate conflict with one another across many situations, and have established a pattern of maladaptive responding that is difficult to break. In view of the recalcitrance of these patterns, the discouraging results that emerged from initial attempts to evaluate the effectiveness of traditional psychotherapeutic approaches to child abuse were somewhat to be expected. Large-scale treatment studies focusing on intrapsychic change in the parent found high recidivism rates of abuse both during and after treatment. Cohn's (1979) evaluation of 11 federally funded demonstration programs indicated that an exceptionally high percentage (30%) of parents reabused their children while treatment was in progress, while Herrenkohl, Herrenkohl, Egolf, & Seech (1979) found a relapse rate of abuse among 66.8% of their 328 treatment families.

In combination with early indications of treatment failure, pressure on the court system and protective service workers to take action to improve the functioning of the family unit was being felt through changes in social viewpoints toward child abuse. A reemphasis on family integrity, as opposed to out-of-home placements, produced less court involvement and fewer and shorter foster-care placements. In response, social service and mental health agencies became more interested in child abuse intervention approaches that were broader in scope than intrapsychic methods, and that would produce changes in parent-child interactions in a shorter time period. Concurrently, behavioral intervention strategies that were effective with other family problems (such as child conduct disorders) were tried with abusive families in an attempt to modify the specific interactional problems identified with each family (see Azar & Wolfe, in press, for discussion of these treatments). These methods were met with initial enthusiasm in view of their emphasis on specific behavioral change and evaluation of treatment effectiveness, and continue to be widely used with abusive populations (Kelly, 1983; Wolfe, Kaufman, Aragona, & Sandler, 1981).

At this point in time, our growing understanding of child abuse, coupled with more suitable intervention methods for dysfunctional families, provides cautious optimism for planning prevention and early intervention programs for this problem. This chapter will focus on recent demonstration projects and ideas favoring the premise that a large proportion of abusive incidents and their associated traumata may be prevented. Undoubtedly, the changes necessary for retooling from a protection to a prevention model of social intervention will offer a considerable challenge. However, the results of recent efforts are encouraging in terms of their potential ramifications for the prevention of childhood victimization.

THE SCOPE OF CHILD ABUSE PREVENTION

Many of the developmental implications of child abuse relate to problems arising from perturbations in the parent-child relationship.

This relationship either was never well established from the beginning (as we saw from the literature on attachment problems among abused children) or it began to disintegrate during periods of developmental change or family stress. Therefore, an overriding goal of child abuse prevention from the perspective of healthy child development is the establishment of positive socialization practices that are responsive to situational and developmental changes. Such healthy practices serve to buffer the child against other socialization pressures that can be stressful or negative, and reduce the need for the parent to rely on power-assertive methods to control the child.

The above-mentioned goal of improving socialization practices is congruent with the transitional model of child abuse presented in Chapter 3. Child abuse seems to arise most often during periods of stressful role transition for parents, such as the postnatal period of attachment, the early childhood period of increasing socialization pressures, times of family instability and disruption (e.g., divorce, single parenthood, change in caregivers), or following chronic detachment from social supports and services. Moreover, we now recognize many of the precursory patterns that accompany a gradual transition toward abusive socialization practices. It is at this juncture that preventive approaches become most sensible for building resistance against many of the unavoidable pressures acting upon high-risk families. The purpose of child abuse prevention therefore involves more than forestalling events that are harmful to the child; prevention can also involve actions that enhance something positive for the child, such as an improved parent-child relationship.

Understandably, questions and doubt arise when considering if a problem as complex as child abuse can be prevented, because it cuts across many different individual, familial, and cultural issues. To be most influential, prevention-oriented approaches to child abuse must propose methods to alter many of the major high-risk factors that have been delineated throughout this book. In global terms, this purpose entails the planning of *competence-promoting strategies* for parents and children that will operate in tandem with efforts for *reducing* the extent and type of *stress* faced by many families. Needless to say, such a long-term and idealistic purpose will inevitably be accompanied by discouragement and frustration on the part of prevention planners unless the goals and objectives are spelled out in a progressive fashion that is carefully matched to individual and cultural interests.

Empirical evidence has been gradually accruing in support of a critical theoretical assumption: Child abuse is a learned behavior that can be conceptualized in social learning terms. The abusive parent often lacks skills for handling life events, personal relationships, and child-rearing responsibilities due more to insufficient learning opportunities and psychological characteristics than to personality disturbances. Optimistically, this notion implies that such behavior can be prevented if appropriate learning opportunities are made available. The goals of prevention therefore involve (1) the development of strong positive habits of child rearing through successful and rewarding parent-child interactions at an early stage of development; (2) improvement in the parent's abilities to cope with stress through exposure to a mental health support system; and (3) the development of the child's adaptive behaviors that will contribute to his or her emotional and psychological adjustment (Wolfe, 1985b). Accordingly, approaches to prevention, early intervention, and treatment should emphasize education and guidance in a format that is flexible and responsive to individual needs (Cohn, 1982).

Rosenberg and Reppucci (1985) suggest several possibilities for child abuse prevention that fit well with the transitional and developmental emphasis noted earlier. They stress that primary prevention programs need to focus on different levels of involvement that are suspected to cause this problem, such as individual, family, and community levels. Prevention efforts must further determine how to address the most critical factors needing attention. An overview of this task, separated into two major issues, is provided below: (a) target selection and timing (When to Prevent What Problems With Whom?), and (b) choice of prevention/intervention methods (Methods of Prevention).

When to Prevent What Problems With Whom?

A pattern of multiple interventions seems to be emerging as the choice for primary or secondary prevention with children who are at risk of developing serious maladjustments. The vast majority of these multiple interventions are aimed at strengthening protective factors in the child's environment rather than focusing directly on aspects of the child's behavior. These protective factors can be grouped into three types of prevention-intervention efforts that (1) modify deleterious characteristics of the target person or family members, (2) reduce family discord and increase the acceptance of the child, or (3) bring into play external agencies to provide a support system for the child and his or her family (Masten & Garmezy, 1985). The timing of such efforts is linked accordingly to the developmental level and needs of the child and family, such as prior to or during transition to parenthood, at pre- and postnatal periods, or upon recognition or admission of problems in the family.

The majority of efforts expended toward child abuse prevention and intervention has been similarly directed toward individuals or environments that are responsible for children's socialization. Although we may wonder why the abused child has not been the direct recipient of much of these efforts, the rationale for providing assistance for parents is very straightforward: Successful attempts to deal with the difficulties of child rearing enhance both the adult's and child's resiliency to the myriad effects of disadvantage and risk. Admittedly, this is a very tall order to fulfill. Yet because child abuse is viewed as an interaction between excessive situational demands and parental ability to withstand adversity, approaches to the problem should focus on ways of reducing demands and enhancing competencies. In effect, any experience of success and mastery on the parent's part—be it employment, social contacts, or pleasing child behavior—is likely to have a powerful impact on child abuse prevention. Likewise, reductions in child-related pressures and demands via subsidized day care and preschools, homemaker programs, and stimulation programs should facilitate the parent's mastery of events that can easily become overwhelming. Therefore, a major challenge of prevention becomes the identification and selection of appropriate, desirable, and attainable goals that can be addressed through community action programs, individual skills-training efforts, and related therapeutic activities.

Drawing upon the major factors associated with child abuse that have been discussed throughout this book, Table 6.1 summarizes the targets for child abuse prevention and intervention in relation to individual, familial, community, and societal levels of involvement. As shown, the majority of these targets fall at the individual level, such as poor coping skills, ineffective child-rearing approaches, longstanding psychological problems, and others. However, this emphasis on the individual should not be interpreted as a reflection of the disproportionate weight that should be given to individuals as opposed to other aspects of the system. It could easily be argued, for example, that interventions effectively reducing the adverse influence on families of socioeconomic conditions (such as subsidized housing and job training programs) can have a significant impact on child abuse prevention as well.

TABLE 6.1
Multilevel Targets for Child Abuse Prevention and Intervention

I. *Individual Level*
   • Psychological problems associated with the parent's history of abusive and/or rejecting childhood experiences
   • Limited coping skills of caregivers
   • Stress-related symptoms affecting emotional and physical health
   • Negative attributions for child transgressions
   • Insensitivity to, or neglect of, child's needs and abilities
   • Low self-esteem, poor self-motivation, limited social competence
   • Limited financial and household management skills
   • Child symptoms associated with victimization (fears, affect disturbance, poor peer relations)

II. *Familial Level*
   • Marital discord and conflict, poor problem-solving abilities
   • Low rate of positive interactions between family members
   • Difficult behavior of child

III. *Community Level*
   • Socioeconomic conditions
   • Support and educational services for disadvantaged families
   • Suitable employment opportunities

IV. *Societal and Cultural Level*
   • Acceptance of corporal punishment of children
   • Low priority for parenthood education and preparation
   • Unequal burden of child-rearing responsibilities placed on women

Methods of Prevention

Child abuse interventions can be aimed at influencing large populations of people in order to reduce the probability of future abuse or they may focus more narrowly on subgroups of individuals who have been identified as "at risk" of developing abusive family patterns due to their background (e.g., an abusive childhood) or current situational factors (e.g., multiple sources of stress). The former approach is based on the premise of primary prevention, whereby methods to enhance overall psychological well-being and strengthen individual competencies and coping resources are offered on a communitywide or large-scale basis. The latter approach relates to the notion of early intervention (i.e., secondary prevention) that is aimed at remediating existing problems in the parent-child relationship that may be precursors to maltreatment. Discussed below are several primary and secondary prevention strategies that hold promise for reducing the incidence and the impact of child abuse and related forms of child maltreatment.

Primary prevention approaches. These programs are most often targeted at the community or societal level of involvement in an attempt to influence large numbers of people in significant aspects of child abuse. Rosenberg & Reppucci (1985) provide three examples of primary child abuse prevention strategies: (1) competency enhancement, such as parent education programs, (2) interventions that prevent the onset of abusive behavior, such as public awareness and information services, and (3) interventions that target vulnerable populations during periods of transition and stress, such as parent-aide and family support programs. These three strategies are summarized in Table 6.2 in reference to their target populations, their timing, and behaviors often targeted for preventive benefit.

Broad-scale efforts to enhance parental competency in large segments of the population offer a relatively inexpensive method for disseminating knowledge of child rearing. Such programs are usually delivered to large audiences or groups in a format that is engaging and/or entertaining, such as the use of live theater, television, or school classrooms. By soliciting the interest of the general public or identified cultural groups, programs with this philosophy can impart information on different parenting methods (e.g., the use of nonviolent punishment), child development (e.g., what to expect of small children) and coping strategies (e.g., seeking advice from others) that is especially relevant for the transition to parenthood. Programs aimed at preventing the onset of abusive behavior, in comparison, focus more upon increasing the general public's awareness and understanding of child maltreatment. These methods include a variety of delivery formats, such as media campaigns, crisis and referral services for families, and community networks that provide support and feedback to families.

Interventions that target vulnerable populations—such as single and teen-aged parents, families of low socioeconomic status or isolated families—and parents undergoing crises offer considerable assistance to these subgroups during pre- and postnatal periods and times of excessive stress. At the level of primary prevention, such efforts are exemplified by local programs that assist identified high-risk families during transitional periods, such as hospital-based programs for improving early parent-child attachment, in-home parent-aides that model effective parenting methods and provide child-rearing assistance, and trained health visitors that sensitize parents to the health and psychological needs of their children.

TABLE 6.2
Approaches to Primary Prevention of Child Abuse

Method	Target Population	Timing of Program	Target Behaviors	Examples of Content
Competency enhancement	General public; specific cultural groups; first-time parents and teens	Prior to or during transition to parenthood	Parenting skills, child development information; coping strategies	Use of live theater and TV to impart parenting information to public
Public awareness campaigns; networking; crisis and referral services	General public; special census tracts or disadvantaged populations	Not necessarily linked to transitional periods	Understanding child abuse and how to seek help	Operation of community crisis lines; strengthening formal and informal helping networks
Family support programs for high-risk groups	Single and teen parents; low SES or isolated families; parents of handicapped children; parents undergoing crises	Pre- and postnatal periods; crisis periods	Parent-child attachment; prenatal health habits and visits to well-child clinics; positive child rearing; home safety	Parent aide is assigned to visit parents at risk in order to assist during transitional periods with advice, transportation

Primary prevention approaches clearly offer several important advantages to dealing with child abuse, which must be weighed in relation to the limited evidence of their effectiveness. Most significantly, these prevention formats are innovative, engaging, and seemingly cost-effective as a means of imparting knowledge and increasing awareness of parental responsibilities. However, in their review of evaluation efforts, Rosenberg and Reppucci (1985) conclude that, with the possible exception of the health visitor concept, the degree to which these approaches can actually prevent child abuse or enhance family functioning is yet unknown. Although primary prevention activities certainly merit a concerted effort, it should be noted as well that such approaches may be too far removed from the time of actual stress, or may not be specific enough to assist those individuals who are in greatest need of assistance in parenting. Additional intervention services, such as those discussed below, are also necessary prevention activities.

Early intervention and treatment approaches. Several intervention strategies have been developed to remediate major deficiencies in parenting skill, knowledge, or coping methods among the more seriously distressed subgroups of families. In contrast to primary prevention, these approaches are most often targeted at the individual and family level of involvement and incorporate delivery formats (that is, group and individual sessions) that are congruent with each family's needs and progress. Treatment components primarily include parent- and family-centered approaches, such as child management training, parent education and support groups, anger and stress management, and methods for treating conditions in the family that precipitate abusive episodes. Although much less common, child-centered treatment or early intervention approaches are also emerging in conjunction with family-centered efforts.

Table 6.3 summarizes the forementioned approaches to early intervention and treatment of child abuse in reference to target populations, timing, and behaviors targeted for intervention. What stands out among the four parent- and family-centered approaches is their focus on particular skill or knowledge deficits among somewhat overlapping target populations. With the possible exception of parent education and support groups, these approaches are intended to modify existing or formative patterns that are highly problematic for the parent and child. For example, parents who require concrete demonstration of methods to promote child compliance, are socially isolated, and/or demonstrate

TABLE 6.3

Approaches to Child Abuse Early Intervention and Treatment

Method	Target Population	Timing of Program	Target Behaviors	Examples of Content
Parent and Family-Centered Approaches				
Child management training	Parents with serious conflict with child; parents requiring concrete demonstration and rehearsal	Early childhood; upon referral to clinic	Effective parenting skills, for example, positive reinforcement, attending, commands, affect and voice tone; nonviolent discipline methods	Therapist demonstrates for parent how to use social and tangible rewards for positive child behavior
Parent education and support groups	Socially isolated; parents in need of group support, information, and sharing of feelings	Transition to parenthood; following crises or self-referral	Understanding of parental responsibilities and different approaches to child rearing; self-esteem; social skills and competence	Community resource person speaks to group about services for small children
Anger and stress management	Self- and court-referred parents demonstrating anger-control problems	Upon recognition or admission of problem	Excessive anger, arousal, impulse-control problems; inappropriate coping reactions	Parent is taught to use positive imagery or relaxation while dealing with a difficult child
Treatment of antecedent conditions in the family	Any family member(s) with major psychological or health-related problems	Upon recognition or admission of problem	Stress-related health problems; marital problems or violence; financial problems related to job skills, and so on	Paraprofessionals or therapists conduct marital counseling, relating to issues that affect parenting
Child-Centered Approaches				
Developmental stimulation	Children showing delays in major developmental areas; parents who show inadequate stimulation	Infancy, toddlerhood, and early childhood	Expressive and receptive language; compliance; sensory-motor development; attachment	Therapist demonstrates visual, auditory, and tactile activities with child; parent imitates
Consultation with school, day-care, or foster-care settings	Children who may present problems across different settings and placements	Upon recognition; at start of new placements	Aggression, social isolation; peer problems; academic delays	Professional meets with teacher and others to suggest ways of improving child's behavior

anger control problems are offered individual or group intervention that is designed to teach such skills as the use of positive reinforcement, nonviolent discipline methods, social skills, and self-control. In some instances a parent may receive assistance in only one of these areas, whereas others may be provided with a multicomponent intervention plan covering several critical needs in progressive or selected stages (see, for example, Lutzker, 1983; Wolfe, Sandler, & Kaufman, 1981).

Child-centered early intervention approaches are much less common than those focusing on needs of the parent and family, even though the importance of involving the child directly in activities to stimulate development and adaptive behavior has a strong basis in the child abuse literature. A child who does not express positive affect, moderate activity level, or age-appropriate language or social skills, for example, may negatively influence the type of care he or she receives. As well, such delays may further impair the child's adaptive abilities at subsequent developmental stages.

Wolfe, Edwards, Manion, and Koverola (in press) report on a recent program for young families identified by child welfare agencies as "at risk" that exemplifies ways of blending parent-centered training with efforts aimed at stimulating the children's adaptive functioning. In addition to parents receiving behavioral training (e.g., teaching positive reinforcement, ignoring, commands, and appropriate punishment; see Forehand & McMahon, 1981), therapists show parents how to engage in daily activities with their children that serve to strengthen children's areas of deficiency and promote their healthy adaptation. These activities include modeling and rehearsal of developmentally appropriate language abilities (e.g., eye contact, responding to simple sounds or phrases, etc.) and social interactional abilities (e.g., following simple directions, engaging in play with the parent, expressing affection and needs). Thus the purpose of training is twofold: to establish beneficial skills and positive child-rearing experiences for the parent and to establish a strong foundation for the development of the adaptive abilities of the child. In conjunction with supportive services from other agencies (e.g., crisis relief, counseling, peer group meetings), this early intervention program has found several desirable improvements in parent-child relations (e.g., fewer reports of child behavior problems, improvements in disruptive child behavior and parenting skills, developmental gains) relative to a control group receiving agency supervision (Wolfe & Manion, 1984; Wolfe et al., in press).

Questions certainly remain as to whom services should be offered and upon what target behaviors early intervention and treatment programs should focus. Interventions based on skills training, for example, seem to be very valuable treatment components (for details of treatment see Isaacs, 1982; Kelly, 1983; Azar & Wolfe, in press), but the success of such training may depend upon the availability of additional support services, such as social networks, child care, and crisis relief. A prevention-oriented approach to child abuse must also contend with the challenge of preventing areas of potential conflict that are not currently problematic. For example, mothers of very young children may not be interested in learning about effective disciplinary methods until such time that their own methods have failed. Equally troublesome are the number of abuse reports involving caregivers that are not invested in the child or who pose an additional risk to the mother and child, such as violent boyfriends or husbands.

Finally, we need to be sensitive to the need to recognize carefully the persons who may benefit from skills training and those who may not. This population is extremely diverse in their needs, and not all will "fit" into a training program or benefit over time. These issues may require a new model or paradigm to approach the complexity of severe parenting problems, since the view that all child abusers are alike has not been supported. The prevention of child abuse, in the final analysis, should encourage diversity and opportunities for the development of unique resources among children and parents.

REFERENCES

Aber, J. L., & Cicchetti, D. (1984). The socio-emotional development of maltreated children: An empirical and theoretical analysis. In H. Fitzgerald, B. Lester, & M. Yogman (Eds.), *Theory and research in behavioral pediatrics* (vol. 2, pp. 147-199). New York: Plenum.

Abramson, L. Y., Seligman, M.E.P., & Teasdale, J. D. (1978). Learned helplessness in humans: Critique and reformulation. *Journal of Abnormal Psychology, 87,* 49-74.

Achenbach, T., & Edelbrock, C. (1981). Behavioral problems and competencies reported by parents of normal and disturbed children aged four through sixteen. *Monographs of the Society for Research in Child Development, 46* (188).

Ainsworth, M.D.S. (1980). Attachment and child abuse. In G. Gerbner, C. J. Ross, & E. Zigler (Eds.), *Child abuse: An agenda for action* (pp. 35-47). New York: Oxford University Press.

Alvy, K. T. (1975). Preventing child abuse. *American Psychologist, 30,* 921-928.

American Humane Association. (1984). *Trends in child abuse and neglect: A national perspective.* Denver, CO: Author.

Appelbaum, A. S. (1977). Developmental retardation in infants as a concomitant of physical child abuse. *Journal of Abnormal Child Psychology, 5,* 417-423.

Aronfreed, J. (1968). *Conduct and conscience: The socialization of internal controls over behavior.* New York: Academic Press.

Atwater, J. B., & Morris, E. K. (1979). *Implications of child effects research for behavioral application.* Paper presented at the annual meeting of the American Psychological Association, New York.

Averill, J. R. (1983). Studies on anger and aggression: Implications for theories of emotion. *American Psychologist, 38,* 1145-1160.

Azar, S. T., Robinson, D. R., Hekimian, E., & Twentyman, C. T. (1984). Unrealistic expectations and problem-solving ability in maltreating and comparison mothers. *Journal of Consulting and Clinical Psychology, 52,* 687-691.

Azar, S. T., & Wolfe, D. A. (in press). Behavioral intervention with abusive families. In E. J. Mash & R. A. Barkley (Eds.), *Behavioral treatment of childhood disorders.* New York: Guilford.

Baldwin, A. L. (1948). Socialization and the parent-child relationship. *Child Development, 19,* 127-136.

Bandura, A. (1973). *Aggression: A social learning analysis.* Englewood Cliffs, NJ: Prentice-Hall.

Barahal, R. M., Waterman, J., & Martin, H. P. (1981). The social cognitive development of abused children. *Journal of Consulting and Clinical Psychology, 49,* 508-516.

Bauer, W. D., & Twentyman, C. T. (1985). Abusing, neglectful, and comparison mothers' responses to child-related and non-child-related stressors. *Journal of Consulting and Clinical Psychology, 53,* 335-343.

Baumrind, D. (1971). Current patterns of parental authority. *Developmental Psychology Monographs, 4*(1, Pt. 2).

Baumrind, D., & Black, A. E. (1967). Socialization practices associated with dimensions of competence in preschool boys and girls. *Child Development, 38,* 291-327.

Bell, G. (1973). Parents who abuse their children. *Canadian Psychiatric Association Journal, 18,* 223-228.

Bell, R. Q., & Harper, L. (1977). *Child effects on adults.* Hillsdale, NJ: Lawrence Erlbaum.

Belsky, J. (1980). Child maltreatment: An ecological integration. *American Psychologist, 35,* 320-335.

Belsky, J. (1984). The determinants of parenting: A process model. *Child Development, 55,* 83-96.

Berkowitz, L. (1974). Some determinants of impulsive aggression. *Psychological Review, 81,* 165-174.

Berkowitz, L. (1983). Aversively stimulated aggression: Some parallels and differences in research with animals and humans. *American Psychologist, 38,* 1135-1144.

Besharov, D. J. (1982). Toward better research on child abuse and neglect: Making definitional issues an explicit methodological concern. *Child Abuse & Neglect, 5,* 383-390.

Blumberg, M. L. (1974). Psychopathology of the abusing parent. *American Journal of Psychotherapy, 28,* 21-29.

Bousha, D. M., & Twentyman, C. T. (1984). Mother-child interactional style in abuse, neglect, and control groups: Naturalistic observations in the home. *Journal of Abnormal Psychology, 93,* 106-114.

Bower, G. H. (1981). Mood and memory. *American Psychologist, 36,* 129-148.

Bradley, E. J. (1986). *A comparison of parental attributions and punitiveness in samples of abusive and nonabusive mothers.* Unpublished doctoral dissertation, Queen's University, Kingston, Ontario.

Bronfenbrenner, U. (1977). Toward an experimental ecology of human development. *American Psychologist, 52,* 513-531.

Brown, G. W., & Harris, T. (1978). *Social origins of depression: A study of psychiatric disorder in women.* London: Tavistock.

Browne, A., & Finkelhor, D. (1986). Impact of child sexual abuse: A review of the literature. *Psychological Bulletin, 99,* 66-77.

Brunnquell, D., Crichton, L., & Egeland, B. (1981). Maternal personality and attitude in disturbances of child rearing. *American Journal of Orthopsychiatry, 51,* 680-691.

Burgess, R. L. (1979). Child abuse: A social interactional analysis. In B. B. Lahey & A. E. Kazdin (Eds.), *Advances in clinical child psychology* (vol. 2, pp. 142-172). New York: Plenum.

Burgess, R. L. (1985). Social incompetence as a precipitant to and consequence of child maltreatment. *Victimology: An International Journal, 10,* 72-86.

Burgess, R. L., & Conger, R. (1978). Family interactions in abusive, neglectful, and normal families. *Child Development, 49,* 1163-1173.

Burgess, R. L., & Youngblade, L. (in press). Social incompetence and intergenerational transmission of abusive parental practices. In R. J. Gelles, G. T. Hotaling, D. Finkelhor, & M. A. Straus (Eds.), *New directions in family violence research.* Newbury Park, CA: Sage.

Caffey, J. (1946). Multiple fractures in the long bones of infants suffering from chronic subdural hematoma. *American Journal of Roentgenology, 56,* 163-173.

Caplan, P. (1986). Take the blame off mother. *Psychology Today, 20,* 70-72.

Cicchetti, D., & Rizley, R. (1981). Developmental perspectives on the etiology, intergenerational transmission, and sequelae of child maltreatment. In D. Cicchetti & R. Rizley (Eds.), *New directions for child development: Developmental perspectives on child maltreatment* (pp. 31-55). San Francisco: Jossey-Bass.

Clarke-Stewart, K. (1978). Popular primers for parents. *American Psychologist, 33,* 359-369.

Cohn, A. H. (1979). Essential elements of successful child abuse and neglect treatment. *Child Abuse & Neglect, 3,* 491-496.

Cohn, A. H. (1982). Stopping abuse before it occurs: Different solutions for different population groups. *Child Abuse & Neglect, 6,* 473-483.

Conger, R. D., Burgess, R., & Barrett, C. (1979). Child abuse related to life change and perceptions of illness: Some preliminary findings. *Family Coordinator, 28,* 73-78.

Coopersmith, S. (1967). *The antecedents of self-esteem.* San Francisco: W. H. Freeman.

Crittenden, P. M. (1985). Maltreated infants: Vulnerability and resistance. *Journal of Child Psychology and Psychiatry, 26,* 85-96.

Crittenden, P. M., & Bonvillian, J. D. (1984). The relationship between maternal risk status and maternal sensitivity. *American Journal of Orthopsychiatry, 54,* 250-262.

Cutrona, C. E. (1984). Social support and stress in the transition to parenthood. *Journal of Abnormal Psychology, 93,* 378-390.

Dietrich, K. N., Starr, R. H., & Kaplan, M. G. (1980). Maternal stimulation and care of abused infants. In T. M. Field, S. Goldberg, D. Stern, & A. M. Sostek (Eds.), *High-risk infants and children: Adult and peer interactions* (pp. 25-41). New York: Academic Press.

Dinkmeyer, D., & McKay, G. D. (1982). *The parent's handbook: Systematic Training for Effective Parenting.* Circle Pines, MN: American Guidance Service.

Disbrow, M. A., Doerr, H., & Caulfield, C. (1977). Measuring the components of parents' potential for child abuse and neglect. *Child Abuse & Neglect, 1,* 279-296.

Dodge, K. A., & Frame, C. L. (1982). Social cognitive biases and deficits in aggressive boys. *Child Development, 53,* 620-635.

Dodge, K. A., Murphy, R. R., & Buchsbaum, K. (1984). The assessment of intention-cue detection skills in children: Implications for developmental psychopathology. *Child Development, 55,* 163-173.

Dohrenwend, B. (1978). Social stress and community psychology. *American Journal of Community Psychology, 6,* 1-14.

Dumas, J., & Wahler, R. G. (1985). Indiscriminate mothering as a contextual factor in aggressive-oppositional child behavior: "Damned if you do, damned if you don't." *Journal of Abnormal Child Psychology, 13,* 1-17.

Egeland, B., Breitenbucher, M., & Rosenberg, D. (1980). Prospective study of the significance of life stress in the etiology of child abuse. *Journal of Consulting and Clinical Psychology, 48,* 195-205.

Egeland, B., & Farber, E. A. (1984). Infant-mother attachment: Factors related to its development and changes over time. *Child Development, 55,* 753-771.

Egeland, B., & Sroufe, L. A. (1981). Attachment and early maltreatment. *Child Development, 52,* 44-52.

Egeland, B., & Vaughn, B. (1981). Failure of "bond formation" as a cause of abuse, neglect, and maltreatment. *American Journal of Orthopsychiatry, 51,* 78-84.

Elmer, E. (1963). Identification of abused children. *Children, 10,* 180-184.

Emery, R. (1982). Interparental conflict and the children of discord and divorce. *Psychological Bulletin, 92,* 310-330.

Epstein, A. S. (1980). *Assessing the child development information needed by adolescent parents with very young children* (Project Report). Ypsilanti, MI: High/Scope Educational Research Foundation.

Erickson, M. T. (1982). *Child psychopathology* (2nd ed.). Englewood Cliffs, NJ: Prentice-Hall.

Feshbach, S. (1980). Child abuse and the dynamics of human aggression and violence. In G. Gerbner, C. J. Ross, & E. Zigler (Eds.), *Child abuse: An agenda for action* (pp. 48-60). New York: Oxford University Press.

Finkelhor, D. (1984). *Child sexual abuse: New theory and research.* New York: Free Press.

Fisher, S. H. (1958). Skeletal manifestations of parent-induced trauma in infants and children. *Southern Medical Journal, 51,* 956-960.

Folkman, S. (1984). Personal control and stress and coping processes: A transactional analysis. *Journal of Personality and Social Psychology, 46,* 839-852.

Forehand, R. L., & McMahon, R. J. (1981). *Helping the noncompliant child: A clinician's guide to parent training.* New York: Guilford.

Friedman, R., Sandler, J., Hernandez, M., & Wolfe, D. (1981). Child abuse. In E. J. Mash & L. G. Terdal (Eds.), *Behavioral assessment of childhood disorders* (pp. 221-255). New York: Guilford.

Friedrich, W. N., & Boriskin, J. A. (1976). The role of the child in abuse: A review of the literature. *American Journal of Orthopsychiatry, 46,* 580-590.

Friedrich, W. N., Einbender, A. J., & Luecke, W. J. (1983). Cognitive and behavioral characteristics of physically abused children. *Journal of Consulting and Clinical Psychology, 51,* 313-314.

Frodi, A. M., & Lamb, M. E. (1980). Child abusers' responses to infant smiles and cries. *Child Development, 51,* 238-241.

Frodi, A., & Smetana, J. (1984). Abused, neglected, and nonmaltreated preschoolers' ability to discriminate emotions in others: The effects of IQ. *Child Abuse & Neglect, 8,* 459-465.

Gaensbauer, T. J., & Sands, K. (1979). Distorted affective communication in abused/neglected infants and their potential impact on caretakers. *Journal of the American Academy of Child Psychiatry, 18,* 236-250.

Gaines, R., Sandgrund, A., Green, A. H., & Power, E. (1978). Etiological factors in child maltreatment: A multivariate study of abusing, neglecting, and normal mothers. *Journal of Abnormal Psychology, 87,* 531-540.

Garbarino, J. (1976). A preliminary study of some ecological correlates of child abuse: The impact of socioeconomic stress on mothers. *Child Development, 47,* 178-185.

Garbarino, J. (1977). The human ecology of child maltreatment: A conceptual model for research. *Journal of Marriage and the Family, 39,* 721-735.

Garbarino, J., & Crouter, A. (1978). Defining the community context of parent-child relations: The correlates of child maltreatment. *Child Development, 49,* 604-616.

Garbarino, J., & Stocking, S. H. (1980). *Protecting children from abuse and neglect.* San Francisco: Jossey-Bass.

Garmezy, N. (1983). Stressors of childhood. In N. Garmezy & M. Rutter (Eds.), *Stress, coping, and development in children* (pp. 43-84). New York: McGraw-Hill.

Gelfand, D., & Peterson, L. R. (1985). *Child development and psychopathology.* Newbury Park, CA: Sage.

Gelles, R. J. (1973). Child abuse as psychopathology: A sociological critique and reformulation. *American Journal of Orthopsychiatry, 43,* 611-621.

Gelles, R. J. (1983). An exchange/social control theory. In D. Finkelhor, R. J. Gelles, G. T. Hotaling, & M. A. Straus (Eds.), *The dark side of families* (pp. 151-165). Newbury Park, CA: Sage.

Gelles, R. J., & Straus, M. A. (1979). Determinants of violence in the family: Toward a theoretical integration. In W. R. Burr, R. Hill, F. I. Nye, & I. L. Reiss (Eds.), *Contemporary theories about the family* (pp. 549-581). New York: Free Press.

Gemeinhardt, M. R. (1986). *A causal modeling approach to parental functioning and children's adjustment.* Unpublished doctoral dissertation, University of Western Ontario, London, Ontario.

George, C., & Main, M. (1979). Social interactions of young abused children: Approach, avoidance, and aggression. *Child Development, 50,* 306-318.

Gil, D. G. (1970). *Violence against children: Physical child abuse in the United States.* Cambridge, MA: Harvard University Press.

Giovannoni, J. M., & Becerra, R. M. (1979). *Defining child abuse.* New York: Free Press.

Green, A. H. (1976). A psychdynamic approach to the study and treatment of child-abusing parents. *Journal of the Academy of Child Psychiatry, 15,* 414-429.

Green, A. H. (1978). Child abuse. In B. B. Wolman, J. Egan, & A. Ross (Eds.), *Handbook of treatment of mental disorders in childhood and adolescence* (pp. 430-455). Englewood Cliffs, NJ: Prentice-Hall.

Green, A. H. (1983). Dimensions of psychological trauma in abused children. *Journal of the American Academy of Child Psychiatry, 22,* 231-237.

Green, A. H., Gaines, R. W., & Sandgrund, A. (1974). Child abuse: Pathological syndrome of family interaction. *American Journal of Psychiatry, 131,* 882-886.

Harter, S. (1983). Developmental perspectives on the self-system. In E. M. Hetherington (Ed.), *Handbook of child psychology* (vol. IV, pp. 275-385). New York: John Wiley.

Helfer, R. E. (1973). The etiology of child abuse. *Pediatrics, 51,* 777.

Herrenkohl, E. C., Herrenkohl, R. C., Toedter, L., & Yanushefski, A. M. (1984). Parent-child interactions in abusive and non-abusive families. *Journal of the American Academy of Child Psychiatry, 23,* 641-648.

Herrenkohl, R. C., Herrenkohl, E. C., & Egolf, B. P. (1983). Circumstances surrounding the occurrence of child maltreatment. *Journal of Consulting and Clinical Psychology, 51,* 424-431.

Herrenkohl, R. C., Herrenkohl, E. C., Egolf, B. P., & Seech, M. (1979). The repetition of child abuse. How frequently does it occur? *Child Abuse & Neglect, 3,* 67-72.

Herzberger, S. D., Potts, D. A., & Dillon, M. (1981). Abusive and nonabusive parental treatment from the child's perspective. *Journal of Consulting and Clinical Psychology, 49,* 81-90.

Hetherington, E. M., Cox, M., & Cox, R. (1979). Play and social interaction in children following divorce. *Journal of Social Issues, 35,* 26-49.

Hoffman, M. L. (1970). Moral development. In P. H. Mussen (Ed.), *Carmichael's manual of child psychology* (vol. 2, pp. 261-359). New York: John Wiley.

Hoffman, M. L. (1975). Moral internalization, parental power and the nature of parent-child internalization. *Developmental Psychology, 11,* 228-239.

Hoffman-Plotkin, D., & Twentyman, C. T. (1984). A multimodal assessment of behavioral and cognitive deficits in abused and neglected preschoolers. *Child Development, 55,* 794-802.

Isaacs, C. D., (1982). Treatment of child abuse: A review of the behavioral interventions. *Journal of Applied Behavior Analysis, 15,* 273-294.

Jaffe, P., Wolfe, D. A., Telford, A., & Austin, G. (1986). The impact of police charges in incidents of wife abuse. *Journal of Family Violence, 1,* 37-49.

Jaffe, P., Wolfe, D. A., Wilson, S., & Zak, L. (1986a). Emotional and physical health problems of battered women. *Canadian Journal of Psychiatry, 31,* 625-629.

Jaffe, P., Wolfe, D. A., Wilson, S., & Zak, L. (1986b). Family violence and child adjustment: A comparative analysis of girls' and boys' behavioral symptoms. *American Journal of Psychiatry, 143,* 74-77.

Janoff-Bulman, R., & Frieze, I. H. (1983). A theoretical perspective for understanding reactions to victimization. *Journal of Social Issues, 39,* 1-17.

Johnson, J. H., & Sarason, I. G. (1978). Life stress, depression, and anxiety: Internal-external control as a moderator variable. *Journal of Psychosomatic Research, 22,* 205-208.

Kadushin, A., & Martin, J. A. (1981). *Child abuse: An interactional event.* New York: Columbia University Press.

Kagan, J. (1983). Stress and coping in early development. In N. Garmezy & M. Rutter (Eds.), *Stress, coping, and development in children* (pp. 191-216). New York: McGraw-Hill.

Kaplan, F. K., Eichler, L. S., & Winickoff, S. A. (1980). *Pregnancy, birth, and parenthood.* San Francisco: Jossey-Bass.

Kazdin, A. E., Moser, J., Colbus, D., & Bell, R. (1985). Depressive symptoms among physically abused and psychiatrically disturbed children. *Journal of Abnormal Psychology, 94,* 298-307.

Kelly, J. A. (1983). *Treating abusive families: Intervention based on skills training principles.* New York: Plenum.

Kempe, C. H. (1973). A practical approach to the protection of the abused child and the rehabilitation of the abusing parent. *Pediatrics, 51,* 804-812.

Kempe, C. H., & Helfer, R. E. (1972). *Helping the battered child and his family.* Philadelphia: Lippincott.

Kempe, C. H., Silverman, F. N., Steele, B. F., Droegenmueller, W., & Silver, H. K. (1962). The battered child syndrome. *Journal of the American Medical Association, 181,* 17-24.

Kilpatrick, D. G., Best, C. L., & Veronen, L. J. (1978). The adolescent rape victim. In K. K. Kreutner & D. R. Hollingsworth (Eds.), *Adolescent obstetrics and gynecology* (pp. 325-357). New York: Yearbook Medical.

Kinard, E. M. (1980). Emotional development in physically abused children. *American Journal of Orthopsychiatry, 50,* 686-696.

Kinard, E. M. (1982). Experiencing child abuse: Effects on emotional adjustment. *American Journal of Orthopsychiatry, 52,* 82-91.

Knutson, J. F. (1978). Child abuse as an area of aggression research. *Journal of Pediatric Psychology, 3,* 20-27.

Kravitz, R. I., & Driscoll, J. M. (1983). Expectations for childhood development among child-abusing and non-abusing parents. *American Journal of Orthopsychiatry, 53,* 336-344.

Lahey, B. B., Conger, R. D., Atkeson, B. M., & Treiber, F. A. (1984). Parenting behavior and emotional status of physically abusive mothers. *Journal of Consulting and Clinical Psychology, 52,* 1062-1071.

Lamb, M. E. (1978). Influence of the child on marital quality and family interaction during the prenatal, perinatal, and infancy periods. In R. M. Lerner & G. Spanier (Eds.), *Child influences on marital and family interaction: A life-span perspective* (pp. 137-163). New York: Academic Press.

Langmeier, J., & Matejcek, Z. (1975). *Psychological deprivation in childhood.* New York: Halstead.

LaRose, L., & Wolfe, D. A. (1987). Psychological characteristics of parents who abuse or neglect their children. In B. B. Lahey & A. E. Kazdin (Eds.), *Advances in clinical child psychology* (vol. 10). New York: Plenum.

Larrance, D. T., & Twentyman, C. T. (1983). Maternal attributions and child abuse. *Journal of Abnormal Psychology, 92,* 449-457.

Lazarus, R. S. (1981). The stress and coping paradigm. In C. Eisdoefer, D. Cohen, A. Kleinman, & P. Maxim (Eds.), *Models for clinical psychopathology* (pp. 177-214). New York: Spectrum Press.

Lefcourt, H. M. (1973). The function of the illusions of control and freedom. *American Psychologist, 28,* 417-425.

Levine, S. (1983). A psychobiological approach to the ontogeny of coping. In N. Garmezy & M. Rutter (Eds.), *Stress, coping, and development in children* (pp. 107-131). New York: McGraw-Hill.

Lewis, D. O., Pincus, J. H., & Glaser, G. H. (1979). Violent juvenile delinquents: Psychiatric, neurological, psychological, and abuse factors. *Journal of the American Academy of Child Psychiatry, 18,* 307-319.

Lewis, M., Feiring, C., McGuffog, C., & Jaskir, J. (1984). Predicting psychopathology in six-year-olds from early social relations. *Child Development, 55,* 123-136.

Light, R. (1973). Abused and neglected children in America: A study of alternative policies. *Harvard Educational Review, 43,* 556-598.

Lipsett, L. (1983). Stress in infancy: Toward understanding the origins of coping behavior. In N. Garmezy & M. Rutter (Eds.), *Stress, coping, and development in children* (pp. 161-190). New York: McGraw-Hill.

Loeber, R., Weissman, W., & Reid, J. (1983). Family interactions of assaultive adolescents, stealers, and nondelinquents. *Journal of Abnormal Child Psychology, 11,* 1-14.

Lorber, R., Felton, D. K., & Reid, J. (1984). A social learning approach to the reduction of coercive processes in child abusive families: A molecular analysis. *Advances in Behavior Research and Therapy, 6,* 29-45.

Lutzker, J. R. (1983). Project 12-Ways: Treating child abuse and neglect from an ecobehavioral perspective. In R. F. Dangel & R. A. Polster (Eds.), *Parent training: Foundations of research and practice.* New York: Guilford.

Lytton, H. (1980). *Parent-child interaction: The socialization process observed in twin and singleton families.* New York: Plenum.

Maccoby, E. E. (1983). Social-emotional development and response to stressors. In N. Garmezy & M. Rutter (Eds.), *Stress, coping, and development in children* (pp. 217-234). New York: McGraw-Hill.

Maccoby, E. E., & Martin, J. A. (1983). Socialization in the context of the family: Parent-child interaction. In E. M. Hetherington (Ed.), *Handbook of child psychology* (vol. IV, pp. 1-101). New York: John Wiley.

Magnuson, E. (1983). Child abuse: The ultimate betrayal. *Time,* pp. 16-18.

Main, M., & George, C. (1985). Responses of abused and disadvantaged toddlers to distress in agemates: A study in the day care setting. *Developmental Psychology, 21,* 407-412.

Martin, J. A., Maccoby, E. E., Baran, K. W., & Jacklin, C. N. (1981). The sequential analysis of mother-child interaction at 18 months: A comparison of microanalytic methods. *Developmental Psychology, 17,* 146-157.

Mash, E. J., Johnston, C., & Kovitz, K. (1983). A comparison of the mother-child interactions of physically abused and non-abused children during play and task situations. *Journal of Clinical Child Psychology, 12,* 337-346.

Masten, A. S., & Garmezy, N. (1985). Risk, vulnerability, and protective factors in developmental psychopathology. In B. B. Lahey & A. E. Kazdin (Eds.), *Advances in clinical child psychology* (vol. 8, pp. 1-52). New York: Plenum.

Maurer, A. (1974). Corporal punishment. *American Psychologist, 29,* 614-626.

McCord, J. (1979). Some childrearing antecedents of criminal behavior in adult men. *Journal of Personality and Social Psychology, 37,* 1477-1486.

McCord, J. (1983). A forty year perspective on effects of child abuse and neglect. *Child Abuse and Neglect, 7,* 265-270.

Melnick, B., & Hurley, J. R. (1969). Distinctive personality attributes of child-abusing mothers. *Journal of Consulting and Clinical Psychology, 33,* 746-749.

Merrill, E. J. (1962). Physical abuse of children: An agency study. In V. DeFrancis (Ed.), *Protecting the battered child.* Denver, CO: American Humane Association.

Milner, J. S., & Wimberley, R. C. (1980). Prediction and explanation of child abuse. *Journal of Clinical Psychology, 36,* 875-884.

Mitchell, R., & Trickett, E. (1980). Task force report: Social networks as mediators of social support. *Community Mental Health Journal, 16,* 27-44.

Morris, M., & Gould, R. (1963). Role reversal: A necessary concept in dealing with the battered child syndrome. *American Journal of Orthopsychiatry, 33,* 298-299.

Mulhern, R. K., & Passman, R. H. (1979). The child's behavioral pattern as a determinant of maternal punitiveness. *Child Development, 50,* 815-820.

National Institute of Mental Health. (1977). *Child abuse and neglect programs: Practice and theory.* Washington, DC: Government Printing Office.

National Center on Child Abuse and Neglect. (1981). *Study findings: National study of the incidence and severity of child abuse and neglect* (DHHS publication No. OHDS 81-30325). Washington, DC: Government Printing Office.

Oldershaw, L. (1986). *A behavioral approach to the classification of different types of physically abusive mothers.* Manuscript submitted for publication, University of Toronto.

Oldershaw, L., Walters, G. C., & Hall, D. K. (1986). Control strategies and noncompliance in abusive mother-child dyads: An observational study. *Child Development, 57,* 722-732.

Pamenter-Potvin, N. (1985). Physical abuse. In D. J. Besharov (Ed.), *Child abuse and neglect law: A Canadian perspective* (pp. 1-27). Washington, DC: Child Welfare League of America.

Parke, R. D. (1977). Socialization into child abuse: A social interactional perspective. In J. L. Tapp & F. J. Levine (Eds.), *Law, justice, and the individual in society: Psychological and legal issues* (pp. 183-199). New York: Holt, Rinehart, & Winston.

Parke, R. D., & Collmer, C. W. (1975). Child abuse: An interdisciplinary analysis. In E. M. Hetherington (Ed.), *Review of child development research* (vol. 5, pp. 509-590). Chicago: University of Chicago Press.

Parke, R. D., & Slaby, R. G. (1983). The development of aggression. In E. M. Hetherington (Ed.), *Handbook of child psychology* (vol. IV, pp. 547-641). New York: John Wiley.

Patterson, G. R. (1982). *Coercive family process.* Eugene, OR: Castalia.

Pelton, L. H. (1978). Child abuse and neglect: The myth of classlessness. *American Journal of Orthopsychiatry, 48,* 608-617.

Perry, M. A., Doran, L. D., & Wells, E. A. (1983). Developmental and behavioral characteristics of the physically abused child. *Journal of Clinical Child Psychology, 12,* 320-324.

Peterson, C., & Seligman, M.E.P. (1983). Learned helplessness and victimization. *Journal of Social Issues, 39,* 103-116.

Polansky, N. A., Chalmers, M., Buttenweiser, E., & Williams, D. (1981). *Damaged parents: An anatomy of child neglect.* Chicago: University of Chicago Press.

Quinton, D., & Rutter, M. (1976). Early hospital admissions and later disturbances of behavior: An attempted replication of Douglas' findings. *Developmental Medicine and Child Neurology, 18,* 447-459.

Radbill, S. X. (1968). A history of child abuse and infanticide. In R. E. Helfer & C. H. Kempe (Eds.), *The battered child* (pp. 3-17). Chicago: University of Chicago Press.

Radke-Yarrow, M., Zahn-Waxler, C., & Chapman, M. (1983). Children's prosocial dispositions and behavior. In E. M. Hetherington (Ed.), *Handbook of child psychology* (vol. IV, pp. 469-545). New York: John Wiley.

Reid, J. B., Taplin, P., & Lorber, R. (1981). A social interactional approach to the treatment of abusive families. In R. B. Stuart (Ed.), *Violent behavior: Social learning approaches to prediction, management, and treatment* (pp. 83-101). New York: Brunner/Mazel.

Reidy, T. J. (1977). The aggressive characteristics of abused and neglected children. *Journal of Clinical Psychology, 33,* 1140-1145.

Rosenberg, M. S., & Reppucci, N. D. (1983). Abusive mothers: Perceptions of their own children's behavior. *Journal of Consulting and Clinical Psychology, 51,* 674-682.

Rosenberg, M. S., & Reppucci, N. D. (1985). Primary prevention of child abuse. *Journal of Consulting and Clinical Psychology, 53,* 576-585.

Rotenberg, K. J. (1980). Children's use of intentionality in judgments of character and disposition. *Child Development, 51,* 282-284.

Rutter, M. (1983). Stress, coping, and development: Some issues and some questions. In N. Garmezy & M. Rutter (Eds.), *Stress, coping, and development in children* (pp. 1-41). New York: McGraw-Hill.

Rutter, M., & Garmezy, N. (1983). Developmental psychopathology. In E. M. Hetherington (Ed.), *Handbook of child psychology* (vol. IV, pp. 775-911). New York: John Wiley.

Salzinger, S., Kaplan, S., & Artemyeff, C. (1983). Mothers' personal social networks and child maltreatment. *Journal of Abnormal Psychology, 92,* 68-76.

Salzinger, S., Kaplan, S., Pelcovitz, D., Samit, C., & Kreiger, R. (1984). Parent and teacher assessment of children's behavior in child maltreating families. *Journal of the American Academy of Child Psychiatry, 23,* 458-464.

Sandgrund, A., Gaines, R. W., & Green, A. H. (1974). Child abuse and mental retardation: A problem of cause and effect. *Journal of Mental Deficiency, 79,* 327-330.

Schneider-Rosen, K., & Cicchetti, D. (1984). The relationship between affect and cognition in maltreated infants: Quality of attachment and the development of visual self-recognition. *Child Development, 55,* 648-658.

Shantz, D. W., & Voyandoff, D. A. (1973). Situational effects on retaliatory aggression at three age levels. *Child Development, 44,* 149-153.

Shaw-Lamphear, V. S. (1985). The impact of maltreatment on children's psychosocial adjustment: A review of the research. *Child Abuse & Neglect, 9,* 251-263.

Silver, R. L., Boon, C., & Stones, M. H. (1983). Searching for meaning in misfortune: Making sense of incest. *Journal of Social Issues, 39,* 81-102.

Silverman, F. N. (1953). The roentgen manifestations of unrecognized skeletal trauma in infants. *American Journal of Reontgenology, 69,* 413-426.

Simpson, K. (1967). The battered baby problem. *Royal Society of Health Journal, 87,* 168-170.

Sloan, M. P., & Meier, J. H. (1983). Typology for parents of abused children. *Child Abuse & Neglect, 7,* 443-450.

Smetana, J., Kelly, M., & Twentyman, C. (1984). Abused, neglected, and nonmaltreated children's judgments of moral and social transgressions. *Child Development, 55,* 277-287.

Smith, J. E. (1984). Non-accidental injury to children—I: A review of behavioral interventions. *Behaviour Research and Therapy, 22,* 331-347.

Smith, S. M., Hanson, R., & Noble, S. (1974). Social aspects of the battered baby syndrome. *British Journal of Psychiatry, 125,* 568-582.

Spinetta, J. J. (1978). Parental personality factors in child abuse. *Journal of Consulting and Clinical Psychology, 46,* 1409-1414.

Spinetta, J. J., & Rigler, D. (1972). The child abusing parent: A psychological review. *Psychological Bulletin, 77,* 296-304.

Sroufe, L. A., & Fleeson, J. (1987). Attachment and the construction of relationships. In W. W. Hartup & Z. Rubin (Eds.), *Relationships and development.* New York: Cambridge University Press.

Sroufe, L. A., & Rutter, M. (1984). The domain of developmental psychopathology. *Child Development, 55,* 17-29.

Standing Senate Committee on Health, Welfare, & Science. (1980). *Child at risk.* Hull, Quebec: Minister of Supply and Services, Canada.

Starr, R. H., Jr. (1979). Child abuse. *American Psychologist, 34,* 872-878.

Starr, R. H., Jr. (1982). A research-based approach to the prediction of child abuse. In R. H. Starr, Jr. (Ed.), *Child abuse prediction: Policy implications* (pp. 105-134). Cambridge, MA: Ballinger.

Steele, B. J., & Pollock, C. (1968). A psychiatric study of parents who abuse infants and small children. In R. Helfer & C. H. Kempe (Eds.), *The battered child* (pp. 89-133). Chicago: University of Chicago Press.

Stevens-Long, J. E. (1973). The effect of behavioral context on some aspects of adult disciplinary practice and effort. *Child Development, 44,* 476-484.

Straker, G., & Jacobson, R. S. (1981). Aggression, emotional maladjustment, and empathy in the abused child. *Developmental Psychology, 17,* 762-765.

Straus, M. A. (1980a). Stress and child abuse. In C. H. Kempe and R. E. Helfer (Eds.), *The battered child* (3rd ed., pp. 86-102). Chicago: University of Chicago Press.

Straus, M. A. (1980b). Victims and aggressors in marital violence. *American Behavioral Scientist, 23,* 681-704.

Straus, M. A., Gelles, R. J., & Steinmetz, S. (1980). *Behind closed doors: Violence in the American family.* Garden City, NY: Doubleday/Anchor.

Susman, E. J., Trickett, P. K., Iannotti, R. J., Hollenbeck, B. E., & Zahn-Waxler, C. (1985). Child-rearing patterns in depressed, abusive, and normal mothers. *American Journal of Orthopsychiatry, 55,* 237-251.

Tarter, R. E., Hegedus, A. E., Winsten, N. E., & Alterman, A. I. (1984). Neuropsychological, personality, and familial characteristics of physically abused delinquents. *Journal of the American Academy of Child Psychiatry, 23,* 668-674.

Toro, P. A. (1982). Developmental effects of child abuse: A review. *Child Abuse and Neglect, 6,* 423-431.

Trickett, P. K., & Kuczynski, L. (1986). Children's misbehaviors and parental discipline strategies in abusive and nonabusive families. *Developmental Psychology, 22,* 115-123.

Tsai, M., Feldman-Summers, S., & Edgar, M. (1979). Childhood molestation: Variables related to differential impacts on psychological functioning in adult women. *Journal of Abnormal Psychology, 88,* 407-417.

Vasta, R. (1982). Physical child abuse: A dual component analysis. *Developmental Review, 2,* 164-170.

Vasta, R., & Copitch, P. (1981). Simulating conditions of child abuse in the laboratory. *Child Development, 52,* 164-170.

Veronen, L. J., & Kilpatrick, D. G. (1980). Self-reported fears of rape victims: A preliminary investigation. *Behavior Modification, 4,* 383-396.

Wahler, R. G. (1980). The insular mother: Her problems in parent-child treatment. *Journal of Applied Behavior Analysis, 13,* 207-219.

Wahler, R. G., & Hann, D. M. (1984). The communication patterns of troubled mothers: In search of a keystone in the generalization of parenting skills. *Education and Treatment of Children, 7,* 335-350.

Wallerstein, J. S., & Kelly, J. B. (1981). *Surviving the breakup: How children and parents cope with divorce.* New York: Basic Books.

Wasserman, S. (1967). The abused parent of the abused child. *Children, 14,* 175-179.

Williams, G.J.R. (1983). Child abuse reconsidered: The urgency of authentic prevention. *Journal of Clinical Child Psychology, 12,* 312-319.

Wolfe, D. A. (1985a). Child abusive parents: An empirical review and analysis. *Psychological Bulletin, 97,* 462-482.

Wolfe, D. A. (1985b). Prevention of child abuse through the development of parent and child competencies. In R. J. McMahon & R. DeVries Peters (Eds.), *Childhood disorders: Behavioral-developmental approaches* (pp. 195-217). New York: Brunner/ Mazel.

Wolfe, D. A. (in press). Child abuse and neglect. In E. J. Marsh & L. G. Terdal (Eds.), *Behavioral assessment of childhood disorders* (2nd ed.). New York: Guilford.

Wolfe, D. A., Edwards, B., Manion, I. G., & Koverola, C. (in press). Early intervention for child abuse and neglect: A preliminary investigation. *Journal of Consulting and Clinical Psychology.*

Wolfe, D. A., Fairbank, J., Kelly, J. A., & Bradlyn, A. S. (1983). Child abusive parents' physiological responses to stressful and nonstressful behavior in children. *Behavioral Assessment, 5,* 363-371.

Wolfe, D. A., Jaffe, P. J., Wilson, S. K., & Zak, L. (1985). Children of battered women: The relation of child behavior to family violence and maternal stress. *Journal of Consulting and Clinical Psychology, 53,* 657-665.

Wolfe, D. A., Kaufman, K., Aragona, J., & Sandler, J. (1981). *The child management program for abusive parents.* Winter Park, FL: Anna.

Wolfe, D. A., & Manion, I. G. (1984). Impediments to child abuse prevention: Issues and directions. *Advances in Behavior Research and Therapy, 6,* 47-62.

Wolfe, D. A., & Mosk, M. D. (1983). Behavioral comparisons of children from abusive and distressed families. *Journal of Consulting and Clinical Psychology, 51,* 702-708.

Wolfe, D. A., Sandler, J., & Kaufman, K. (1981). A competency-based parent training program for abusive parents. *Journal of Consulting and Clinical Psychology, 49,* 633-640.

Wolfe, V. V., & Wolfe, D. A. (in press). The sexually abused child. In E. J. Mash & L. G. Terdal (Eds.), *Behavioral assessment of childhood disorders* (2nd ed.). New York: Guilford.

Wright, L. (1976). The "sick but slick" syndrome as a personality component of parents of battered children. *Journal of Clinical Psychology, 32,* 41-45.

Young, L. (1964). *Wednesday's children: A study of child neglect and abuse.* New York: McGraw-Hill.

Zahn-Waxler, C., Cummings, E. M., McKnew, D. H., & Radke-Yarrow, M. (1984). Altruism, aggression, and social interactions in young children with a manic-depressive parent. *Child Development, 55,* 112-122.

Zajonc, R. B. (1980). Feeling and thinking: Preferences need no inferences. *American Psychologist, 35,* 151-175.

Zillman, D. (1979). *Hostility and aggression.* Hillsdale, NJ: Lawrence Erlbaum.

AUTHOR INDEX

SUBJECT INDEX

ABOUT THE AUTHOR

David A. Wolfe (Ph.D., University of South Florida) is Associate Professor of Psychology at the University of Western Ontario, where he teaches in the subspecialty area of clinical child psychology. He is a Diplomate in Clinical Psychology from the American Board of Professional Psychology, and has an active consulting practice with the Children's Aid Society of Ontario and the London Family Court Clinic. His research involves understanding and preventing the effects on children of physical and sexual abuse and exposure to chronic family violence. His editorial board memberships have included *Child Abuse & Neglect, Journal of Family Violence, Journal of Consulting and Clinical Psychology,* and the *Journal of Clinical Child Psychology.* He is coauthor, with K. Kaufman, J. Aragona, and J. Sandler, of *The Child Management Program for Abusive Parents.*

NOTES

NOTES

NOTES